Essential Maths Skills for

A-L ...try

Love it or lo... A-Levels
— witho... uch.

Not to worry. ...ly to meet
during the cou... w it works.

We've also inclu... e got to grips
with everything. ...of a sudden...

A-Level revision? It has to

Published by CGP

Editors:
Mary Falkner, Robin Flello, Emily Howe, Paul Jordin and Sophie Scott.

ISBN: 978 1 78294 472 0

With thanks to Barrie Crowther for the proofreading.
With thanks to Jan Greenway for the copyright research.

Cover Photo **Laguna Design**/Science Photo Library

Clipart from Corel®
Printed by Elanders Ltd, Newcastle upon Tyne.

Based on the classic CGP style created by Richard Parsons.

Contents

Words that are highlighted in **orange** are defined in the Glossary.

Using a Scientific Calculator

Knowing your way around a calculator will make the mathsy bits of chemistry a lot more straightforward, so grab yourself a scientific calculator and hold on tight...

Get Familiar With How Your **Calculator** Works

Depending on the calculator you have, these buttons might look a bit different or be in different places, but they'll work in the same way.

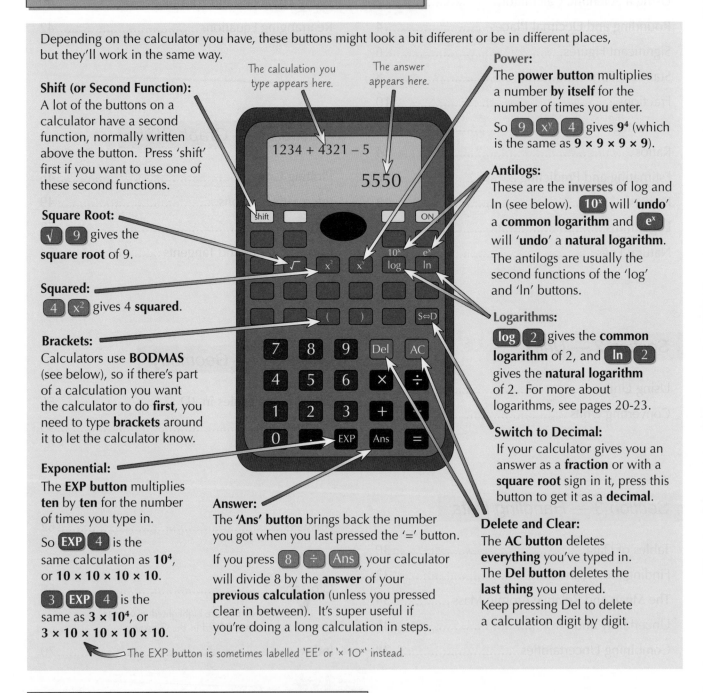

The calculation you type appears here.

The answer appears here.

1234 + 4321 − 5

5550

Shift (or Second Function):
A lot of the buttons on a calculator have a second function, normally written above the button. Press 'shift' first if you want to use one of these second functions.

Square Root:
√ 9 gives the **square root** of 9.

Squared:
4 x^2 gives 4 **squared**.

Brackets:
Calculators use **BODMAS** (see below), so if there's part of a calculation you want the calculator to do **first**, you need to type **brackets** around it to let the calculator know.

Exponential:
The **EXP button** multiplies **ten** by **ten** for the number of times you type in.

So EXP 4 is the same calculation as 10^4, or 10 × 10 × 10 × 10.

3 EXP 4 is the same as 3 × 10^4, or 3 × 10 × 10 × 10 × 10.

↰ The EXP button is sometimes labelled 'EE' or 'x 10^x' instead.

Answer:
The **'Ans' button** brings back the number you got when you last pressed the '=' button.

If you press 8 ÷ Ans, your calculator will divide 8 by the **answer** of your **previous calculation** (unless you pressed clear in between). It's super useful if you're doing a long calculation in steps.

Power:
The **power button** multiplies a number **by itself** for the number of times you enter.
So 9 x^y 4 gives 9^4 (which is the same as **9 × 9 × 9 × 9**).

Antilogs:
These are the **inverses** of log and ln (see below). 10^x will '**undo**' a **common logarithm** and e^x will '**undo**' a **natural logarithm**. The antilogs are usually the second functions of the 'log' and 'ln' buttons.

Logarithms:
log 2 gives the **common logarithm** of 2, and ln 2 gives the **natural logarithm** of 2. For more about logarithms, see pages 20-23.

Switch to Decimal:
If your calculator gives you an answer as a **fraction** or with a **square root** sign in it, press this button to get it as a **decimal**.

Delete and Clear:
The **AC button** deletes **everything** you've typed in. The **Del button** deletes the **last thing** you entered. Keep pressing Del to delete a calculation digit by digit.

Calculators do Things in a **Fixed Order**

You need to be careful entering calculations into a calculator — there's a set order that they always work in.

1) First they'll work out anything in **brackets**.
2) Next they'll work out any **powers** or **roots** (this is called a number's **order**). Any **logarithms** are included in this step, too.
3) Then they'll do any **division** or **multiplication**.
4) The last things they'll work out are the **additions** and **subtractions**.

You can remember this order as **BODMAS** — **B**rackets, **O**rder, **D**ivision and **M**ultiplication, **A**ddition and **S**ubtraction.

Be **really careful** about remembering to put brackets in where you need them to make sure you get the right answer.

Using a Scientific Calculator

Worked Example

Leo types these three calculations into his calculator:

a) $10 - 3 \times 4 + 4^2$ b) $(10 - 3) \times (4 + 4^2)$ c) $(10 - 3 \times 4 + 4)^2$

What answer does he get for each calculation? Show why the answers are different.

1 *Type each calculation into your calculator and press the 'equals' button to find the answer.*

a) $10 - 3 \times 4 + 4^2 = \mathbf{14}$    This is what you'd type into your calculator.

b) $(10 - 3) \times (4 + 4^2) = \mathbf{140}$

c) $(10 - 3 \times 4 + 4)^2 = \mathbf{4}$

2 *Use BODMAS to show why the answers are different.*

Remember, the order for calculations is **B**rackets, **O**rder, **D**ivision and **M**ultiplication, **A**ddition and **S**ubtraction.

a)   This calculation has no brackets, so the first thing the calculator does is sort out orders (powers) by doing 4^2.
The next step is the multiplication, so the next thing the calculator does is find 3×4.
Finally, the calculator does the additions and subtractions, in order from left to right.

$$10 - 3 \times 4 + 4^2$$
$$= 10 - 3 \times 4 + 16$$
$$= 10 - 12 + 16 = \mathbf{14}$$

b)   In this calculation there are two sets of brackets.
Inside each set of brackets, the calculator uses the BODMAS order too.
Then the calculator does the multiplication.

$$(10 - 3) \times (4 + 4^2)$$
$$= 7 \times (4 + 16)$$
$$= 7 \times 20 = \mathbf{140}$$

The order of operations can cause a few problems.

c)   In this calculation the calculator works out the brackets first.
Inside the brackets, it does the multiplication first. Then it does the addition and subtraction (working from left to right).
Lastly, the calculator does the 'order' and squares the whole lot.

$$(10 - 3 \times 4 + 4)^2$$
$$= (10 - 12 + 4)^2$$
$$= 2^2 = \mathbf{4}$$

In b) and c), adding in brackets changes the order that the calculator solves the problem.
In both cases, the brackets **change the answer** from a).

> This explains why you need to be **really careful** about where you put the brackets when you're typing a calculation into your calculator — in some places they won't make a difference but in other places they'll have a **big effect** on your answer.

My second function is switching off...

It's not the most thrilling topic in the world, I'll admit, but it's important that you can use all the functions you'll need on your calculator. Make sure you know where all these buttons are and have a go at using them. If you're feeling really daring, you could even see how adding brackets into some calculations changes the answers you get, you maverick...

Rounding and Decimal Places

Often when you do calculations in chemistry, the answer you get on your calculator will have loads of digits after the decimal point. You need to know how to round answers like this to a given number of decimal places.

Rounding **Shortens** Long Numbers

You can **round** long decimals to a set number of decimal places.

For example, the number of moles in a 244.4 g sample of magnesium sulfide is found by the calculation: number of moles = mass ÷ M_r = 244.4 ÷ 56.4

56.4 = M_r of magnesium sulfide

244.4 ÷ 56.4 = **4.33333333333333333333333333333...** mol

As the digits go further to the right, they get smaller in value.

The answer rounded to **ten** digits after the decimal place is: **4.3333333333** mol

The answer rounded to **five** digits after the decimal place is: **4.33333** mol

The answer rounded to **two** digits after the decimal place is: **4.33** mol

You Can Round to a Certain Number of **Decimal Places**

Most of the time, you round your answers to a sensible number of significant figures instead — see pages 6-7.

There are certain types of calculation where the usual practice is to round your answer to a given number of **decimal places** (e.g. when you take the log of a number — see page 20). For example, say you were rounding 8.17633 to 2 decimal places. Here's what you'd do:

1) Find the position of the **last digit** that will be in the rounded number.

1 2 3 4 5
8.17633

Start counting from the decimal point. You're rounding to **two** decimal places, so the last digit will be in the **second** decimal place.

2) Look at the next digit to the **right**. If that digit is **less than 5**, the last digit stays the **same**. If the digit is **5 or more**, round **up** the last digit.

8.17⑥33

The next digit is more than 5, so round the last digit up from 7 to 8.

3) So, 8.17633 rounded to 2 decimal places is: **8.18**

Don't give any more digits after the second decimal place.

Worked Example 1

The pH of a solution is calculated to be 1.049843. **What is the pH to 3 decimal places?**

1 *Find the position of the last digit that will be in the rounded number.*
Start counting from the decimal point. The last digit will be in the third decimal place.

1 2 3
1.049843
The last digit is 9.

2 *Look at the next digit to the right.*
Rounding up a 9 is slightly trickier — the 9 becomes a 0, and the digit to the left of it increases by 1.

The next digit is 8. **1.049⑧43**

8 is more than 5, so round up. The last digit is 9, so 49 gets rounded up to 50.

1.049843 = 1.050 (3 d.p.) ⟵ It's helpful to let anyone reading your answer know how you've rounded it — d.p. stands for decimal places.

Rounding and Decimal Places

Avoid Rounding *Too Early*

If you're doing a calculation with several steps, you should always write out your working.

Whenever possible, keep the exact result of each step in your calculator to use in the next step, instead of using a rounded value. Don't round until the very end of the calculation.

Worked Example 2

A reaction produced 8.25 g of carbon dioxide (M_r = 44.0) in 23 seconds.
Find the rate of reaction in mol min^{-1} to 3 decimal places. Show your working.

number of moles = mass ÷ M_r

1 **Convert the mass to moles.**

The number of moles is mass ÷ M_r.

8.25 ÷ 44.0
0.1875

number of moles = 8.25 ÷ 44.0
= 0.1875

This is an exact decimal, so don't round it — just write it down to use later in the calculation.

2 **Convert the time to minutes.**

Divide by 60 to convert seconds to minutes.

23 ÷ 60
3.833333333

time in minutes = 23 ÷ 60
= 0.3833...

You can't write out the full decimal here because it goes on forever — but these dots show whoever's looking at your working that you haven't rounded yet.

3 **Find the rate.**

The rate is 'number of moles ÷ time'.
Use the calculator's 'Ans' key to divide 0.1875 by the unrounded answer from step 2.

0.1875 ÷ Ans
0.4891304348

rate = 0.1875 ÷ 0.3833...
= 0.48913... mol min^{-1}

4 **Find the position of the last digit that will be in the rounded number.**

Start counting from the decimal point.
The last digit will be in the third decimal place.

The last digit is 9.

1 2 3
0.4891304348

5 **Look at the next digit to the right.**

rate = 0.48913... mol min^{-1}
= **0.489 mol min^{-1} (3 d.p.)**

The next digit is 1.

0.4891304348

1 is less than 5, so the last digit stays the same.

If you'd rounded too early and done 0.188 ÷ 0.383, you'd have ended up with 0.491 mol min^{-1} as your final answer.

Practice Questions

Q1 Write down the following amounts:
a) 0.0272 g s^{-1} to 3 decimal places
b) 11.325 dm^3 to 2 decimal places
c) 23.976 kJ to 1 decimal place
d) 0.9191 V to 2 decimal places

Q2 A certain chemical reaction has one product, which is produced at a rate of 325 g every 80 minutes. Using the formula 'rate = mass ÷ time', find the rate of this reaction in kg hour^{-1}. Give your answer to 2 decimal places.

To convert g to kg, divide by 1000. See pages 27-29 for more on unit conversions.

My sheepdog's no good at maths — he can only round up...

Rounding isn't glamorous, I admit, but it comes in really useful when you end up with an answer that's about as long as your arm. Remember, try not to round any numbers until the end of a calculation, or it might affect your final answer.

Significant Figures

Significant figures might not be the most exciting topic, but you'll need to think about them in pretty much every calculation you do in chemistry, so it's a good idea to get the hang of them.

Almost *All Values* are Given to a Number of *Significant Figures*

Occasionally in chemistry you might come across an **exact value** (usually things you can count that can't be broken down into smaller parts) — e.g. the **number of electrons** orbiting the nucleus of an atom.

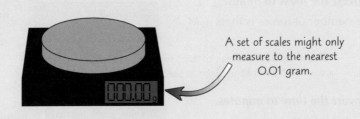

But for most quantities in chemistry it's impossible to make an exact measurement — your method will never be perfect, and there will be a limit to how small a change your equipment can detect.

This measuring cylinder only measures to the nearest 0.2 cm³.

A set of scales might only measure to the nearest 0.01 gram.

A **significant figure** is any digit in a value that you are confident is correct. A non-significant figure is any digit that you can't be sure about. It's important to know how to recognise **how many** significant figures a value you're given has and how to **round** your own data to an appropriate number of significant figures (see next page).

Rounding your answer to an **appropriate** number of **significant figures** is the 'normal' thing to do in a chemistry calculation. You should **always** give your answers to an appropriate number of significant figures unless you've got a **good reason** not to (e.g. if you are using an exact value, or if a question tells you to do something different).

Count the Number of Significant Figures from the *First Non-Zero Digit*

To find the number of **significant figures** (or **s.f.**) a value is given to:

1) **Start** counting at the **first non-zero digit**.
2) **Stop** counting at the **last non-zero digit**, or the last digit after the **decimal point** if there are any.

So: **187.23** s is given to **5** significant figures.
1 2 3 4 5

9.005 kJ is given to **4** significant figures.
1 2 3 4

700 007 cm³ is given to **6** significant figures.
1 2 3 4 5 6

448 000 g is given to **3** significant figures.
1 2 3
Actually, this could be to 4, 5 or 6 s.f. — but unless you know that for certain, you can only assume it's given to 3. See below for more.

Zeros at the *End* of a Number are *Significant* if They Come *After a Decimal Point*

Zeros that come after a decimal point give you **extra information**:

159.0 g is given to **4 significant figures**
1 2 3 4

Using 159 g would give you the same answer in any calculation as 159.0 g, so the fact this zero has been included means it must be **significant**.

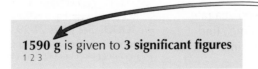

1590 g is given to **3 significant figures**
1 2 3

On the other hand, this final zero **doesn't** tell you anything about how many significant figures the measurement has. You can't tell if the mass was measured as 1590 g to **4 significant figures**, or as e.g. 1592 g and then **rounded** down to 1590 g to **3 significant figures**. You can only be **certain** that it has the **smaller number** of significant figures, so you'd assume it was given to **3 s.f.**.

This is one reason why, when you're writing down a number, you should always put something after it to tell a person looking at it how many significant figures it has been measured to — e.g. 1350 cm³ **(to 4 s.f.)**.

Significant Figures

Zeros at the Start of a Number are Not Significant

Look back at the rule on page 6 — you don't start counting until the first **non-zero** digit.

So: **0.039 m** is given to **2** significant figures.   **0.000701 g** is given to **3** significant figures.

This makes sense if you think about converting the same number into **different units** (see pages 27-29). 0.039 m is the same as 3.9 cm or 0.000039 km — these are all **different ways** of writing the **same information**, so they must all have the same number of **significant figures**.

There's an Important Rule for Significant Figures in Calculations

You should round your final answer to a calculation to the **same number of significant figures** as the data value with the **fewest** significant figures used in the calculation.

1) If you give an answer to **more** significant figures than the data you've used to calculate it, you're saying that your calculated result is **more precise** than the data it came from — so you should stick to using the smallest number of significant figures from your data.

2) The exception to this rule is when you're working with **logarithms** — they have their own rules, which are coming up on page 20.

It's a good idea to write down the **unrounded answer** in your working, then give the **rounded answer** along with the **number of significant figures** you're giving it to.

If you use your answer in another calculation, use the unrounded version.

Worked Example

A reaction was found to have a theoretical yield of 7.65 g. The actual yield was 4.2 g.
Calculate the percentage yield of the reaction using this formula: percentage yield = $\frac{\text{actual yield}}{\text{theoretical yield}} \times 100\%$.

1 **Do the calculation.** $\frac{4.2}{7.65} \times 100\% = 54.90196078...$ Don't round your answer yet.

2 **Look at the significant figures in the question.**
The actual yield is 4.2 g, so it's given to 2 s.f., and the theoretical yield is 7.65 g, so it's given to 3 s.f.

3 **Round your answer.**
The actual yield has the fewest significant figures (2) so the final answer should also be given to 2 significant figures.

9 > 5, so round up.
$54.90196078... = 55\%$ **(to 2 s.f.)**
State how many s.f. your answer is given to.

Practice Questions

Q1 How many significant figures are each of these values given to?
a) 221 985 Pa   b) 15 200 g   c) 39.00 K   d) 0.00186 mol

Q2 What is 649.352 kJ to: a) two significant figures?   b) three significant figures?   c) four significant figures?

Q3 0.175 moles of sodium chloride were dissolved in 1.2 dm³ of water.
Using the formula, 'concentration (mol dm⁻³) = number of moles ÷ volume (dm³)', calculate the concentration of the resulting solution. Give your answer to an appropriate number of significant figures.

I wish my bank balance was a bit more of a significant figure...

The rule about significant figures in calculations is a really important one. It's also going to be used on almost every page of this book, so it's a good idea to get familiar with it. At least it's pretty simple though.

Standard Form

*A lot of numbers that come up in chemistry are written in **standard form**.*

Standard Form Gets **Rid** of Some **Zeros**

Standard form **tidies up** very big or very small numbers in calculations. For example:

1 mole of a substance contains about 602 000 000 000 000 000 000 000 particles
(this number is called the Avogadro constant). In standard form, this is:

In standard form, this number is always between 1 and 10.

$$6.02 \times 10^{23}$$

This means $6.02 \times 10 \times 10 \times 10 \times 10 \times 10 \times 10$
$\times 10 \times 10 \times 10 \times 10 \times 10 \times 10 \times 10 \times 10$
$\times 10 \times 10 \times 10 \times 10 \times 10 \times 10 \times 10 \times 10$.

pH calculations sometimes use the ionic product of water, K_w.
The value of K_w at 25 °C is 0.000 000 000 000 010 0 mol dm^{-3}. In standard form, you'd write this as:

A negative power means the number is between −1 and 1.

$$1.00 \times 10^{-14} \text{ mol dm}^{-3}$$

Ordinary numbers are sometimes referred to as being written in 'decimal form'.

Numbers in Standard Form Are Written in a **Particular Way**

Numbers in standard form will always look like this:

This number is always between **1** and **10**.

$$A \times 10^n$$

This is the **number of places** the **decimal point** would have to move if you wrote the number out in full.

To covert a number from **decimal form** into **standard form**:

- Put the decimal point after the **first non-zero value** in your number, followed by any other significant figures. This is **A**.
- **Count** how many places the **decimal point** has moved. This is **n**. *n* is **negative** if the decimal point has moved to the **right**, and **positive** if the decimal point has moved to the **left** (so *n* is negative for numbers that are between −1 and 1).

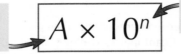

$A = 7.82$

$78\ 200 \text{ Pa} = 7.82 \times 10^4 \text{ Pa}$

The decimal point moves four places to the left, so $n = 4$.

To covert a number from **standard form** into **decimal form**:

- Move the decimal point *n* **places**. It moves to the **left** if *n* is **negative**, and the **right** if *n* is **positive** (the opposite way around from above).

$n = -3$, so move the decimal point 3 places to the left.

$5.1 \times 10^{-3} \text{ m}^3 = 0.0051 \text{ m}^3$

$A = 5.1$

Be careful to keep the number of **significant figures** (see pages 6-7) in your answer the same when you're switching between standard form and decimal form:

- If you knew the pressure on a gas was **3 000 000 Pa to 3 s.f.**, and you wanted to write this in **standard form**, you'd write **3.00×10^6 Pa (to 3 s.f.)** — make sure you include digits for all the significant figures.
- If the enthalpy change of a reaction was given as **9.0×10^5 J mol^{-1} to 2 s.f.**, and you wanted to write this in **decimal form**, you'd write **90 000 J mol^{-1} (to 2 s.f.)**.

You Can Use a **Calculator** to Work With Values in Standard Form

To enter a value in standard form into your calculator, type in the normal part (*A* in the box above), then press either: EXP or $\times 10^x$ or EE depending on your calculator. Then type in the power (*n*).

Your calculator might display a number in standard form like this:

This is the same as **8.61×10^6**.

Standard Form

Worked Example

A chemical plant produces ammonia gas at a rate of 3 360 000 mol h^{-1}.
The plant operates for 12.0 hours each day.

a) **Calculate how many moles of ammonia are produced by the plant each day.
Give your answer in standard form.**

b) **The ammonia produced in one day is stored in a tank with a volume of 1.94×10^6 dm³.
Calculate the concentration of ammonia in the tanks in mol dm⁻³.**

concentration = number of moles ÷ volume

1 *Find the number of moles of ammonia produced each day.*

The plant operates for 12.0 hours a day, so multiply the amount produced per hour by 12.0.

$$12.0 \text{ h} \times 3\ 360\ 000 \text{ mol } h^{-1} = \textbf{40 320 000 mol}$$

2 *Convert the number of moles produced each day into standard form.*

You want to write 40320000 mol in the form $A \times 10^n$.
A needs to be between 1 and 10, so $A = 4.0320000$.
That moves the decimal place 7 places to the left, so $n = 7$.

$$40320000 \text{ mol} = 4.0320000 \times 10^7 \text{ moles}$$
$$= \textbf{4.03} \times \textbf{10}^7 \textbf{ moles (to 3 s.f.)}$$

Give your answer to an appropriate number of significant figures (see pages 7).

The form was so standard, Cliff could fill it in without even looking at it.

3 *Calculate the concentration in the tank.*

You know the tank has a volume of 1.94×10^6 dm³. You can use this value together with the unrounded value for the number of moles from part 2 to calculate the concentration.

$$\text{concentration} = \text{number of moles} \div \text{volume} = (4.0320000 \times 10^7) \div (1.94 \times 10^6) = 20.7835...$$
$$= \textbf{20.8 mol dm}^{-3} \textbf{ (to 3 s.f.)}$$

It would also be fine to write this as 40320000 ÷ (1.94×10^6).

Practice Questions

Q1 The concentration of hydrogen ions in a solution is measured as 0.000 035 mol dm⁻³.
Rewrite this in standard form.

Q2 The pressure in a container of gas is measured as 2.15×10^5 Pa. Rewrite this in decimal form.

Q3 Using the formula 'number of moles = (concentration × volume in cm³) ÷ 1000', find the number of moles of sodium hydroxide in 75 cm³ of 6.3×10^{-5} mol dm⁻³ sodium hydroxide solution.
Give your answer in standard form.

Q4 A reaction produced 6.85×10^{12} dm³ of sulfur dioxide gas.
a) Convert this volume to m³. Give your answer in standard form.
b) Convert this volume to cm³. Give your answer in standard form.

1 m³ = 1000 dm³
1 dm³ = 1000 cm³
(See page 28 for more about these conversions.)

Q5 An atom of sodium has a mass of 3.82×10^{-23} g.
Use this information to calculate the number of atoms in 25 g of sodium.

So, that's standard form — what about deluxe form?

This stuff crops up a lot in AS and A-level chemistry — calculations involving concentrations and moles tend to involve really large numbers of really small things, so standard form will often come in very handy. Fortunately, your calculator will do most of the work for you — but make sure that you understand what's going on, or you could get tripped up.

Fractions

Fractions get everywhere in chemistry — but they aren't half bad. As my American friend said when we were watching The Third Man, "If I had a quarter for every time a fraction had helped me out, I could live on Fifth Avenue..."

Fractions are Divisions

A lot of the **formulas** you'll need in chemistry have **fractions** in them.
A fraction's is just another way to represent a **division**, so:

$$\text{number of moles} = \frac{\text{mass}}{M_r}$$ means $$\text{number of moles} = \text{mass} \div M_r$$

$$R_f = \frac{\text{distance travelled by spot}}{\text{distance travelled by solvent}}$$ means $$R_f = \frac{\text{distance travelled}}{\text{by spot}} \div \frac{\text{distance travelled}}{\text{by solvent}}$$

Remember to Use BODMAS When You're Dealing with Fractions

If your formula is just made up of one **simple fraction**, that's nice and easy.
If it includes a more **complicated fraction**, or if there's a fraction plus some **other stuff** going on too, you'll need to use **BODMAS** (see page 2) to figure out what order to do things in.

- For an expression like $\frac{24}{1.2} + \frac{12}{96}$, the normal **BODMAS rules** apply
  — you do the **divisions** (the fractions) **first**, then add them together.

- $24 \div 1.2 = \textbf{20}$ and $12 \div 96 = \textbf{0.125}$, so $\frac{24}{1.2} + \frac{12}{96} = 20 + 0.125 = \textbf{20.125}$

- You can check this calculation for yourself using your **calculator**.
  You can either do this using the **divide button**...

  (2)(4)(÷)(1)(.)(2)(+)(1)(2)(÷)(9)(6)(=) | 24 ÷ 1.2 + 12 ÷ 96 |
  | 20.125 |

  ...or using the **fraction button** (if you have one).

  If you use the fraction button, your calculator might give you the answer as a fraction. You can convert it to a decimal with the 'switch to decimal' button (see page 2).

There's also an **extra** BODMAS rule you need to know for dealing with more complex fractions — **invisible brackets**.

- For something like $\frac{24 + 12}{1.2 + 96}$, you have to treat the **top** and **bottom** of the fraction as though they've got **invisible brackets** round them.

- That means do **all** the calculations on the **top** and on the **bottom first** — then **divide** top by bottom.

- So this isn't **24 + 12 ÷ 1.2 + 96**. It's **(24 + 12) ÷ (1.2 + 96)**.

- If you try **both versions** on the calculator, you'll see you get **completely different answers**:

  (2)(4)(+)(1)(2)(÷)(1)(.)(2)(+)(9)(6)(=) | 24 + 12 ÷ 1.2 + 96 |
  | 130 | This is **not** equal to $\frac{24+12}{1.2+96}$

  (()(2)(4)(+)(1)(2)())(÷)(()(1)(.)(2)(+)(9)(6)())(=) | (24 + 12) ÷ (1.2 + 96) |
  | 0.3703703704 |

  This **is** the value of $\frac{24+12}{1.2+96}$

Fractions

Worked Example

The percentage atom economy of a reaction is calculated using the formula

$$\% \text{ atom economy} = \frac{\text{molecular mass of desired product}}{\text{sum of molecular masses of all products}} \times 100$$

The main industrial method of making chloromethane produces 1 mole of chloromethane and 1 mole of water for every mole of the reactants used.
The molecular mass of chloromethane is 50.5 and the molecular mass of water is 18.0.
Calculate the atom economy of this method of producing chloromethane.

1 *Put the right values into the formula.*

The desired product is chloromethane.
Its molecular mass, 50.5, goes on the top of the fraction.
The bottom of the fraction is the sum of the molecular masses of chloromethane and water — that's 50.5 + 18.0.

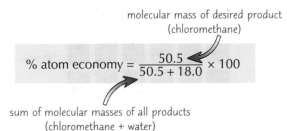

molecular mass of desired product
(chloromethane)

$$\% \text{ atom economy} = \frac{50.5}{50.5 + 18.0} \times 100$$

sum of molecular masses of all products
(chloromethane + water)

2 *Find the value on the bottom of the fraction.*

Expressions on the top and bottom of a fraction have invisible brackets round them, so find 50.5 + 18.0 first.

$$\% \text{ atom economy} = \frac{50.5}{68.5} \times 100$$

50.5 + 18.0 = 68.5

3 *Then do the rest of the calculation.*

Treat the fraction as a division.

$$\% \text{ atom economy} = \frac{50.5}{68.5} \times 100$$
$$= 0.73722... \times 100$$
$$= \textbf{73.7\% (to 3 s.f.)}$$

Practice Questions

Q1 The percentage yield of a reaction is found using the formula 'percentage yield = $\frac{\text{actual yield}}{\text{theoretical yield}} \times 100$'.

Find the percentage yield of a reaction with a theoretical yield of 256.0 g and an actual yield of 187.5 g.

Q2 The following formula can be used to find the number of moles in a given volume of a solution:

number of moles = $\frac{\text{concentration in mol dm}^{-3} \times \text{volume in cm}^3}{1000}$

Use the formula to find the number of moles of sodium hydroxide in 50 cm^3 of 0.020 mol dm^{-3} solution.

Q3 The number of moles of gas in a certain volume can be found using the formula $n = \frac{pV}{RT}$,

where n = number of moles, R = 8.31 J K^{-1} mol^{-1} (the gas constant), T = temperature in K,
p = pressure in Pa and V = volume in m^3.
a) Find the number of moles in 0.50 m^3 of nitrogen gas at a pressure of 160 000 Pa and a temperature of 450 K.
b) Find the number of moles in 0.35 m^3 of carbon dioxide gas at a pressure of 225 000 Pa
and a temperature of 80 °C, given that temperature in K = temperature in °C + 273.

Get in on the fraction action...

Those invisible brackets are an invisible pest. They mean you can't necessarily just bung a fraction formula into your calculator and get the right answer out. The best thing to do is take everything step by step — work out the value of the top and bottom of the fraction separately, then when there's just one number in each, and only then, do the division.

Percentages

Percentages pop up all over the place in real life — and you'll see them quite a lot in chemistry too, so it's worth making sure you understand what they are and how to work with them.

Percentages Help You Compare Parts of Different-Sized Totals

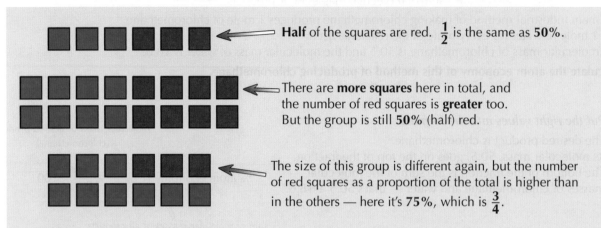

Half of the squares are red. $\frac{1}{2}$ is the same as **50%**.

There are **more squares** here in total, and the number of red squares is **greater** too. But the group is still **50%** (half) red.

The size of this group is different again, but the number of red squares as a proportion of the total is higher than in the others — here it's **75%**, which is $\frac{3}{4}$.

You'll meet **percentages** in a variety of different places in chemistry. For example:
- **Relative abundances** of elements or isotopes in a sample are often given as percentages.
- **Percentage atom economy** measures the percentage of the reactants that end up in useful products.
- **Percentage yield** compares the amount of product formed by a reaction to the amount you'd expect it to form.

Percent Means 'Out of 100'

When you're working with percentages, you'll usually have to multiply or divide a number by one hundred at some point. There are two rules you need to know:

To show one number as a percentage of another:

1) **Divide** the first number by the second...
2) ...then **multiply** the answer by **100**.

6 out of 10 as a percentage is:

$\frac{6}{10} = 6 \div 10 = 0.6$

$0.6 \times 100 = \textbf{60\%}$

To find a percentage of a number:

1) **Divide** the percentage by **100** to get a decimal...
2) ...then **multiply** the number by this decimal.

60% of 10 is:

$60 \div 100 = 0.6$

$0.6 \times 10 = \textbf{6}$

Percentages **don't have any units**.

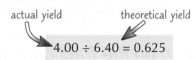

Suddenly, Bernard wasn't 100% sure that pole-vaulting without a pole was really a good idea.

Worked Example 1

A student prepared copper(II) oxide in the lab by heating copper(II) carbonate. He expected the reaction to produce 6.40 g of copper(II) oxide, but in fact it only produced 4.00 g.

The percentage yield of a reaction is calculated using this formula: percentage yield $= \dfrac{\text{actual yield}}{\text{theoretical yield}} \times 100$.

Calculate the percentage yield of this reaction.

1 **Divide the actual yield of the reaction by the theoretical yield.**

The question is asking you to find 4.00 g out of 6.40 g as a percentage — so the first step is to divide 4.00 by 6.40.

actual yield   theoretical yield

$4.00 \div 6.40 = 0.625$

2 **Multiply by 100 to turn the result into a percentage.** $0.625 \times 100 = \textbf{62.5\%}$

Percentages

Percentages Add Up To 100%

Percentages that represent the different parts of a total will all add up to 100%.

For example, if a mixture of gases contains 55% nitrogen, 25% oxygen and the rest is carbon dioxide, then the percentage of carbon dioxide must be 100 – 55 – 25 = **20%**

Worked Example 2

Compound X is composed of carbon, hydrogen and oxygen only. It is found to contain 40% carbon and 6.7% hydrogen by mass.
What percentage of the mass of the compound is oxygen?

1 **Subtract the percentages of carbon and hydrogen from 100%.**
You know that all of the compound is made up of these three elements, and you know the percentages of carbon and hydrogen. Oxygen must be the rest.

100 – 40 – 6.7 = **53.3%**

Worked Example 3

Compound Y is composed of iron and sulfur only. It contains 56.60% iron by mass. A sample of compound Y was found to contain 14.15 g of iron.
What is the mass of sulfur in the sample?

1 **Work out the total mass of the sample.**
Since you know that compound Y contains 56.60% iron by mass, 56.60% of the sample must have a mass of 14.15 g. So to find the mass of the whole sample, divide 14.15 by 56.60 and multiply by 100.

This is 56.60% ÷ 56.60 = 1%...
$(14.15 \div 56.60) \times 100 = 25.00$ g
...so this is 1% × 100 = 100%.

2 **Find the percentage of sulfur in the sample.**
56.60% of the sample is iron and the rest is sulfur. So to find the percentage of sulfur in the sample, take 56.60 away from 100.

100 – 56.60 = 43.40%

3 **Find the mass of sulfur in the sample.**
43.40% of the sample is sulfur and the total mass is 25.00 g. So the mass of sulfur is 43.40% of 25.00 g.

43.40 ÷ 100 = 0.4340
0.4340 × 25.00 = **10.85 g**

You could also do this by subtracting the mass of iron from the total mass of the sample that you found in step 2.

Practice Questions

Q1 A 10.0 g sample of a copper alloy contains 8.80 g of copper.
a) What is the percentage by mass of copper in the alloy?
b) Calculate the mass of copper in a 16.0 g sample of the same alloy.

Percentage by mass just means 'the percentage of the total mass of the compound that's made up of an element'.

Q2 The percentage by mass of carbon in an unidentified hydrocarbon is 85.7%.
a) What is the percentage by mass of hydrogen in the hydrocarbon?
b) A sample of the hydrocarbon contains 24.6 g carbon. What is the total mass of the sample?
c) Another sample of the hydrocarbon has a total mass of 35.0 g. What is the mass of hydrogen in this sample?

Hydrocarbons are compounds which only contain hydrogen and carbon atoms.

70% of people understand percentages — the other 40% don't...

The main thing you need to know about percentages is that they're one part divided by the whole thing, times 100. For example, percentage uncertainty (see page 37) is the uncertainty in a measurement, divided by the total measurement, times 100. Percentage yield is the yield you got, divided by the total yield that you expected, times 100. Smashing.

Ratios

*A **ratio** is just a is way of expressing how much of one thing you have compared to a second thing...*

Ratios are a Way of Comparing Quantities

To write a ratio, you just need to write the number of one thing that you have compared to the number of another thing that you have, separated by a **colon**.

Here, for every **four squares** there are **seven circles**. So the ratio of squares to circles is **4 : 7**.

Now, for every **four squares** there are **six circles**. So the ratio of squares to circles is **4 : 6**. You can also say that for every **two squares** there are **three circles**, so the ratio can also be written as **2 : 3** — this is the **simplest form** of this ratio.

Ratios don't just have to contain two numbers — they can contain as many numbers as there are categories. The ratio of squares to circles to stars below would be written as **4 : 2 : 7**.

Ratios are really important in chemistry, because they're used to write **chemical formulas** and **equations**. For example, you could say that in carbon dioxide (CO_2), the ratio of carbon atoms to oxygen atoms is 1 : 2. Or that in the reaction $2Zn + O_2 \rightarrow 2ZnO$, the ratio of moles of ZnO produced to moles of O_2 used is 2 : 1.

Multiply or Divide to Make Equivalent Ratios

Ratios are usually written like this:

A colon separates one quantity from the other.

x and y stand for the quantities of each thing.

- If you **multiply** or **divide all the numbers** in a ratio by the **same thing**, it's still the **same ratio**.
- Ratios that are the same are called **equivalent ratios**.
- A ratio that's written so it contains the smallest possible **whole numbers** is said to be in its **simplest form**.

These three ratios are all equivalent — they're different ways to write the same ratio.

$$\times 10 \left\{ \begin{array}{c} 40 : 20 \\ 4 : 2 \\ 2 : 1 \end{array} \right\} \times 10$$
$$\div 2 \qquad\qquad \div 2$$

2 : 1 is the ratio in its simplest form.

Worked Example 1

The empirical formula of a compound shows the atoms in the compound in their simplest ratio.
What is the empirical formula of a compound with molecular formula C_8H_{12}?

1 **To simplify the ratio, divide all the numbers by the same thing.**

C_8H_{12} contains C and H in the ratio 8 : 12.

The numbers in the initial ratio both divide by 2...

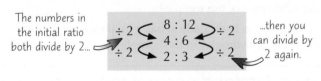

...then you can divide by 2 again.

8 and 12 both divide by 4, so you could do this in one step.

2 **Stop when you can't divide any further.**

You can't simplify the ratio any more, so this gives you the numbers of each atom in the empirical formula.

So the empirical formula of C_8H_{12} is C_2H_3.

Ratios

Worked Example 2

Ammonia (NH_3) can be formed by reacting nitrogen with hydrogen: $N_2 + 3H_2 \rightarrow 2NH_3$
How many moles of H_2 are needed to produce 24.2 moles of ammonia?

1 **Write out the ratio of H_2 to NH_3 from the equation.**
For every 3 moles of hydrogen gas, you get 2 moles of ammonia.

$H_2 : NH_3 = 3 : 2$

2 **Divide both sides of the ratio by 2.**
This gives you an equivalent ratio that tells you how many moles of hydrogen you need to produce 1 mole of ammonia.

$\div 2 \begin{array}{c} 3:2 \\ 1.5:1 \end{array} \div 2$

3 **Multiply both sides of the ratio by 24.2.**
This gives you another equivalent ratio that tells you how many moles of hydrogen you need to produce 24.2 moles of ammonia.

$\times 24.2 \begin{array}{c} 1.5:1 \\ 36.3:24.2 \end{array} \times 24.2$

To produce 24.2 moles of NH_3 you need **36.3 moles** of H_2.

Worked Example 3

A compound is known to contain sulfur and oxygen only. A sample of the compound was found to contain 0.0844 moles of sulfur and 0.253 moles of oxygen.
Find the empirical formula of the compound.

1 **The numbers of moles are a ratio.**
The elements in the compound will always be present in the same ratio as in the empirical formula.

sulfur : oxygen = 0.0844 : 0.253

2 **Simplify the ratio.**
To find the simplest form of the ratio, divide everything by the smallest number — in this case, that's 0.0844.

S: $\frac{0.0844}{0.0844} = 1.00$ O: $\frac{0.253}{0.0844} = 3.00$

The ratio of S : O in the molecule is 1 : 3.

In this example, both sides of the ratio come out as whole numbers. If one bit didn't come out as a whole number, you'd need to multiply to get the ratio in its simplest form — e.g. if it came out as 1 : 1.5, you'd multiply both sides by two to turn it into 2 : 3.

3 **Use the ratio to write the empirical formula.**
Remember, you can just write 'S' rather than 'S_1'.

So the empirical formula is **SO_3**.

Practice Questions

Q1 Glucose has the molecular formula $C_6H_{12}O_6$.
 a) What is the ratio of carbon : hydrogen : oxygen in a molecule of glucose?
 b) What is the empirical formula of glucose?

Q2 A compound has the empirical formula C_2H_4O. Each molecule of this compound contains 3 oxygen atoms. Find its molecular formula.

Q3 A certain reaction produces 3 moles of carbon dioxide for every 4 moles of water produced. In an experiment, the reaction was carried out and 22 moles of water were formed. How many moles of carbon dioxide did the reaction make?

Q4 A scientist analyses a compound containing sulfur, fluorine and chlorine only. A sample of the compound is found to contain 0.0308 moles of sulfur, 0.154 moles of fluorine and 0.0308 moles of chlorine. What is the empirical formula of this compound?

The ratio of maths questions I like to those I don't is 1 : 1000...

Once you've got the hang of the types of question shown on these pages, you might find you can answer them without writing the ratios out — but make sure you follow the underlying maths so you know what you're dealing with.

Estimating and Predicting

When you can't measure or calculate something accurately, estimating can be really handy.

An **Estimate** is an **Approximate Value** of a Quantity

Estimates are useful when it's either **not possible** to be accurate (for example when you're working with something that's **hard to measure** or can't be measured **directly**), or when a rough value is all that's required.

It's helpful if you have an idea of the **size** of the **different units** (see Section 2) that you'll come across in chemistry, so that you can make estimates using them. For example:

$1 dm^3$ = 1 litre
— that's about the same as a carton of orange juice.

100 g is roughly the mass of small apple.

1 gram of carbon contains about 5×10^{22} atoms.

Estimations can be used to help **design experiments**, to make **predictions** about how changing one variable will change another, or to **quickly check** the answer to a calculation to make sure it's in the right ballpark.

Making **Estimates** Can Help You to **Design Sensible Experiments**

1) When you're planning an experiment you'll have to make decisions about what **equipment** and **reagents** to use. For example, what size of gas syringe to use to collect a gas, or what concentration of acid to use.

2) Sometimes it can be useful to make a **rough estimate** of the outcome of your experiment to help you make these decisions. This can help you to design an experiment which is **safe** and will give you **clear**, **accurate results**.

Here's an example:

Choosing an indicator to use for an acid base titration.

1) In an acid-base titration, you add an **indicator**, which **changes colour** at the end point of the titration.

2) Which indicator you use will depend on the **acid** and **base** you're using — you need to pick one that's **appropriate** for your titration. Some examples of indicators and the pH at which they change colour are shown in the table on the right.

Indicator	pH range of colour change
Orange IV	1.4 – 2.6
Bromophenol blue	3.0 – 4.6
Cresol purple	7.6 – 9.2
Phenolphthalein	8.3 – 10.0

3) Imagine you were planning a titration where you gradually added **hydrochloric acid** (a **strong acid**) to **ammonia solution** (a **weak base**). To choose a suitable indicator, you'd need to predict roughly what would happen to the pH of the solution during the titration.

4) One way that you could do this would be to **sketch a pH curve** (a graph that shows how pH changes during a titration) for your experiment, like the one shown below. The **general shape** of the pH curve will be the same when you add any **strong acid** to any **weak base**.

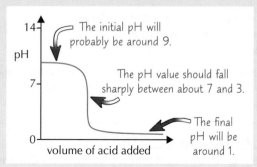

The initial pH will probably be around 9.

The pH value should fall sharply between about 7 and 3.

The final pH will be around 1.

volume of acid added

5) Every indicator has a **pH range** where it changes colour. You need one that will change colour at the point in the experiment where the pH changes **rapidly**. This corresponds to the **steepest part** of the pH curve.

6) Using the sketch graph, you can **estimate** that for the ammonia-hydrochloric acid titration, the pH will change most rapidly between about **pH 7** and **pH 3**.

7) Looking at the table, this suggests **bromophenol blue** would be a suitable indicator for this titration, as it changes colour within the range pH 3 to pH 7.

Estimating and Predicting

Estimation Can Help You Make Predictions

1) **Changing** the value of one of the **variables** in a formula, will cause the value of some of the other variables in the formula to change too.

2) You can **estimate** the **overall effect** that any changes you make will have, and make what's called a **qualitative prediction**. That means you don't try to predict the **actual value** of each variable, but think about things like whether each one will **increase or decrease**, and by **how much**.

Worked Example

The ideal gas equation describes the relationship between the pressure, volume, temperature and number of moles of gas in a system. It can be written in the form $\frac{pV}{nT} = R$, where p = pressure in Pa, V = volume in m^3, n = number of moles, T = temperature in K and $R = 8.31$ J K^{-1} mol^{-1} (the gas constant).

The temperature of a sealed glass jar of pure nitrogen gas is decreased. Use the equation to predict the effect of this change on the pressure, volume and number of moles of gas present.

1 *Think about which numbers have to stay the same.*
- R is a constant, so it's always equal to 8.31 J K^{-1} mol^{-1}. That means that if you change the temperature, some of the other variables must change so that the value of $\frac{pV}{nT}$ stays constant.
- The volume of a sealed jar can't change, so V must stay constant.
- n is also constant, as there's no way for any nitrogen to escape or for more to get in, and nothing for it to react with. So the number of moles must stay the same.

2 *Work out the effect on the numbers that change.*
- You know that V and n must stay the same, so you can work out what will happen to p as T decreases.
- The value of nT will decrease as T decreases, so you'll be dividing pV by a smaller number.
- If you divide by a smaller number, the answer gets bigger (e.g. $1 \div 4 < 1 \div 2$). So to keep the overall value of the fraction the same, the number on the top must decrease.
- So the pressure must decrease when the temperature decreases.

When the temperature of the jar decreases, the pressure also decreases. The volume and number of moles remain the same.

Practice Questions

Q1 A student is planning an experiment to follow the rate of the reaction between hydrochloric acid and sodium carbonate. The mass of the reaction vessel will decrease as carbon dioxide gas is given off, so the student plans to follow the progress of the reaction by recording the mass of the vessel at regular intervals.

a) Based on data for similar experiments, the student estimates that the reaction will take 4 minutes to reach completion. Suggest a suitable time interval that the student could leave between measurements.

b) The student estimates that the total mass lost during the experiment will be just under 2 g. Suggest a suitable level of accuracy for the student's mass measurements.

Q2 Phosphorus(V) chloride decomposes in the following reversible reaction: $PCl_{5(g)} \rightleftharpoons PCl_{3(g)} + Cl_{2(g)}$

The equilibrium constant, K_c, for this reaction is: $\frac{[PCl_3][Cl_2]}{[PCl_5]}$

where [A] = concentration of A in mol dm^{-3}. Predict the effect on the value of K_c of changing the conditions so that less of the PCl_5 dissociates.

In a reversible reaction, changing the conditions can increase the quantities of reactant or products present on one side of the equation (which decreases them on the other side).

Estimating — not the same as guessing...

Don't get sloppy if a question asks you to estimate something — you can't just pull an answer out of thin air. You need to be able to explain the reasoning behind any predictions that you make. For a topic that's about how to find rough answers, this is pretty hard work. Never mind, reward yourself for getting through it with approximately* one biscuit.

*Although how approximately is up to you...

Powers

*A **power** is like an instruction that tells you how many times to multiply a number by itself.*
Make sure you know all the rules for dealing with them.

Powers Show Repeated Multiplication

Powers look like this:

$\overset{\text{base}}{\curvearrowright} a^n \overset{\text{power}}{\curvearrowleft}$

> You might also see the small superscript number being called an exponent or an index.

The small number tells you what **power** the **base** has been **raised to**. Powers can be **positive** or **negative**.

A **positive power** tells you how many times to multiply the base by itself.

$$2^5 = 2 \times 2 \times 2 \times 2 \times 2 = 32$$

2 to the power 5 = 5 lots of 2, all multiplied together

$$10^3 = 10 \times 10 \times 10 = 1000$$

10 to the power 3 = 3 lots of 10, all multiplied together

A **negative power** is the same as a **fraction** that's '1 over the positive version of the power':

$$a^{-n} = \frac{1}{a^n}$$

$$4^{-2} = \frac{1}{4^2} = \frac{1}{4 \times 4} = \frac{1}{16} = 0.0625$$

$$5^{-3} = \frac{1}{5^3} = \frac{1}{5 \times 5 \times 5} = \frac{1}{125} = 0.008$$

Use Your Calculator to Work Out Powers

> It might even look like this: Fancy.

If you wanted to find 4^{10} on your calculator, you'd need the **powers button**.
The powers button on your calculator probably looks like this $\boxed{x^y}$ or like this $\boxed{\wedge}$.
The two versions work in exactly the **same way**.
For 4^{10}, you just enter $\boxed{4}\ \boxed{x^y}\ \boxed{1}\ \boxed{0}\ \boxed{=}$ or $\boxed{4}\ \boxed{\wedge}\ \boxed{1}\ \boxed{0}\ \boxed{=}$.

4^10

1048576

> If you've got a fancy, newish calculator, it might even display this as 4^{10}.

Worked Example 1

For the equilibrium $2H_{2}S_{(g)} + CH_{4(g)} \rightleftharpoons 4H_{2(g)} + CS_{2(g)}$, the gas equilibrium constant, K_p, is given by the formula
$K_p = \dfrac{(p_{H_2})^4 \times p_{CS_2}}{(p_{H_2S})^2 \times p_{CH_4}}$ (where p_A = partial pressure of gas A).

Calculate the value of K_p for this equilibrium when $p_{H_2} = 80$ kPa, $p_{CS_2} = 20$ kPa, $p_{H_2S} = 60$ kPa and $p_{CH_4} = 25$ kPa.

① Put the values into the formula for K_p.
Write out the formula with the numbers in the right places before you
stick it in your calculator, so it's clear you've used the right method.

$$K_p = \frac{80^4 \times 20}{60^2 \times 25}$$

② Use your calculator to work out the powers.
You'll need the $\boxed{x^y}$ or $\boxed{\wedge}$ button to find 80^4.
For 60^2 you can use the $\boxed{x^2}$ to save your little fingers from having to key in the 2.

$$K_p = \frac{40\,960\,000 \times 20}{3600 \times 25}$$

③ Do the multiplications, then the division.
Remember, the top and bottom of a fraction have invisible brackets
round them (see page 10), so do the multiplications first, then divide
top by bottom when they're both single numbers.

$$K_p = \frac{819\,200\,000}{90\,000}$$
$$= 9102.22...$$
$$= 9100 \text{ kPa}^2 \text{ (to 2 s.f.)}$$

The units here are kPa². If you'd like to know why, there's a full
explanation of how units like this are worked out on pages 24-26.

Powers

You Need to Know the Power Laws

These rules all apply to any powers that you find in units as well as in numerical expressions. See Section 2 for more on units.

There are a few **rules** you need to know to make dealing with powers easier. First off, a couple of **special cases**:

Any number **to the power 1** is just the number **itself**: $a^1 = a$ $5^1 = 5$ $2.9814^1 = 2.9814$

Any number **to the power 0** is **1**: $a^0 = 1$ $9^0 = 1$ $185\ 623\ 110^0 = 1$

There are rules for **multiplying** and **dividing** powers that have the same **base** (the number that's being raised to the power) too.

To **multiply** two powers with the **same base**, **add** the powers: $a^n \times a^m = a^{(n+m)}$
E.g. $2^6 \times 2^3 = 2^{6+3} = 2^9 = 512$

To **divide** a power by another power with the **same base**, **subtract** the powers: $a^n \div a^m = a^{(n-m)}$
E.g. $2^6 \div 2^3 = 2^{6-3} = 2^3 = 8$

The most likely place you'll need these rules for multiplying and dividing powers in chemistry is when you're working with numbers in **standard form** (see pages 8-9).

Worked Example 2

1 mole of hydrogen ions contains 6.02×10^{23} ions.
How many hydrogen ions are there in 1 dm³ of a solution which has a hydrogen ion concentration of 1.25×10^{-4} mol dm⁻³?

number of moles = concentration × volume

1 **Find the number of moles of H⁺ ions in 1 dm³ of solution.**
Multiply the concentration of the solution by its volume in dm³ to find how many moles of H⁺ ions are in it.

moles of H⁺ ions = concentration × volume
$= 1.25 \times 10^{-4} \times 1$
$= \mathbf{1.25 \times 10^{-4}}$ **moles**

2 **Write out a calculation that you can use to find the number of ions in 1 dm³ of solution.**
This will mean multiplying the number of moles by the number of H⁺ ions in 1 mole.

number of H⁺ ions
= moles of H⁺ ions × number of ions in 1 mole
$= \mathbf{(1.25 \times 10^{-4}) \times (6.02 \times 10^{23})}$

3 **Rearrange the multiplication.**
If you're just multiplying numbers, you can do them in any order (even if some of them are in brackets).

$(1.25 \times 10^{-4}) \times (6.02 \times 10^{23})$
$= 1.25 \times 6.02 \times 10^{-4} \times 10^{23}$

4 **Do the calculation.**
Pop 1.25 × 6.02 into your calculator, and then use the power rules to sort out the powers of 10.

$1.25 \times 6.02 \times 10^{-4} \times 10^{23} = 7.525 \times 10^{-4} \times 10^{23}$
$= 7.525 \times 10^{(-4+23)}$
$= 7.525 \times 10^{19}$ ions
$= \mathbf{7.53 \times 10^{19}}$ **ions (3 s.f.)**

Practice Questions

Q1 Given that 1 mole of silicon contains 6.02×10^{23} ions, find the number of atoms in 10^5 moles of silicon. Give your answer in standard form.

Q2 The equilibrium constant, K_c, for the reaction $2CH_{4(g)} \rightleftharpoons 3H_{2(g)} + C_2H_{2(g)}$ is given by the formula $K_c = \dfrac{[H_2]^3[C_2H_2]}{[CH_4]^2}$. Calculate the value of K_c if $[H_2] = 0.60$ mol dm⁻³, $[C_2H_2] = 0.20$ mol dm⁻³, and $[CH_4] = 0.40$ mol dm⁻³. (The units of K_c for this reaction are mol² dm⁻⁶.)

Q3 The rate equation for a reaction is rate = $k[A][B]$. At a certain temperature, k was found to be 1.12×10^4 mol⁻² dm⁶ s⁻¹ when $[A] = 1.96 \times 10^{-4}$ mol dm⁻³ and $[B] = 1.84 \times 10^{-2}$ mol dm⁻³. Find the rate of this reaction at this temperature. The units of the rate are mol dm⁻³ s⁻¹.

A pow-er is also any comic book character who hits people a lot...

This is a topic where slick calculator skills come in handy. It's quicker and easier to key in 80^4 than $80 \times 80 \times 80 \times 80$, and anything that can save you precious seconds in an exam is worth getting the hang of. There are plenty of examples to play with on these pages — make sure you that can do them on your own calculator and get the same answers out.

Logarithms

As I'm sure you're aware, one of the great unanswerable questions of our time is "What's the opposite of badger?"
*On the other hand, "What's the opposite of powers?" is very answerable. Time to meet **logarithms**...*

Logarithms Are the Opposite of Powers

When you raise 10 to a power, you can write the calculation like this:

$$10^x = y$$

This means multiply 10 by itself x times.

E.g. $10^3 = 10 \times 10 \times 10 = 1000$

Logarithms (or 'logs') are the **opposite of powers** — or in maths-speak, logs and powers are **inverses** of each other. A logarithm with **base 10** tells you the **power that 10 has been raised to** in order to give that number.

This small number just tells you what the base is.

$$\log_{10} y = x$$

x is the power that ten is raised to make y.

You can take logs with other bases too — see pages 22-23.

$10^4 = 10\,000$
so
$\log_{10} 10\,000 = 4$

$\log_{10} 25 = 1.40$
so
$10^{1.40} = 25$

$10^{-2.92} = 0.0012$
so
$\log_{10} 0.0012 = -2.92$

10 raised to a negative power will give a number that's less than 1...

...so $\log_{10}$ of a number less than 1 is always negative.

Because 10^x and $\log_{10}x$ are **inverse functions**, you can say that $10^{\log_{10}x} = x$ and $\log_{10}(10^x) = x$.
For example, $10^{\log_{10}7} = 7$ and $\log_{10}(10^5) = 5$.

You Can Use Your Calculator to Find the Log of a Number

Your calculator should have a button like this:  log

This will give you the log to **base ten** of whatever number you enter after you press it.
You might need to put **brackets** around whatever you're taking the log of.

You will often see $\log_{10}x$ just written as log x.

Your calculator should also have a button like this: 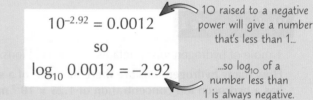 10^x

This will give you ten to the power of whatever number you enter after you press it.

This may be a 'second function' on your calculator, so you may have to press shift or second function first.

Follow These Special Significant Figure Rules When Working with Logs

1) When you're taking the log of a number, you **don't** use the normal significant figures rules on page 7.
   Instead, you should give your answer to the **same number of decimal places** (d.p.)
   as there are **significant figures** (s.f.) in the number you're taking the log of. For example:

There is **1 significant figure** in 0.2.	$\log_{10} 0.2 = -0.69897... = -0.7$ to **1 decimal place**.
There are **2 significant figures** in 3.9×10^8.	$\log_{10} (3.9 \times 10^8) = 8.59106... = 8.59$ to **2 decimal places**.
There are **4 significant figures** in 17.01.	$\log_{10} 17.01 = 1.230704... = 1.2307$ to **4 decimal places**.

2) If you **raise ten** to a power, you should give your answer to the same number of **significant figures**
   as there are **decimal places** in the power. For example:

There is **1 decimal place** in 0.5.	$10^{0.5} = 3.1622... = 3$ to **1 significant figure**.
There are **2 decimal places** in −8.65.	$10^{-8.65} = 2.23872... \times 10^{-9} = 2.2 \times 10^{-9}$ to **2 significant figures**.
There are **3 decimal places** in 4.229.	$10^{4.229} = 16\,943.378... = 16\,900$ to **3 significant figures**.

Logarithms

The pH Scale Uses Logs

The main use of logs in chemistry is the **pH scale**, which is used to compare **hydrogen ion concentrations**.
The formula for pH is:

$$pH = -\log_{10} [H^+]$$

$[H^+]$ = hydrogen ion concentration (in mol dm^{-3})

The pH scale makes it easier to **compare** the acidity of solutions. The hydrogen ion concentration of one solution could be **many thousands of times** greater or smaller than another, but the pH values for both will lie between 0 and 14 (the normal range of the pH scale).

Worked Example 1

What is the pH of a solution of sulfuric acid with a hydrogen ion concentration of 0.13 mol dm^{-3}?

1 *Use the pH formula.*
$[H^+] = 0.13$, so use your calculator to find the pH.

$$pH = -\log_{10} 0.13$$

pH values don't have any units.

2 *Don't forget the special significant figure rules.*
0.13 has 2 significant figures, so give $\log_{10} 0.13$ to 2 decimal places.

$$pH = 0.88605... = \textbf{0.89}$$

Worked Example 2

What is the hydrogen ion concentration of a solution of ammonia with a pH of 7.80?

1 *Rearrange the pH formula.*
10^x and $\log_{10} x$ are inverses of each other, so $[H^+] = 10^{-pH}$.

$$pH = -\log_{10} [H^+]$$
$$\log_{10} [H^+] = -pH$$
$$[H^+] = 10^{-pH}$$

See pages 42-45 for more on how to rearrange equations like this.

2 *Use the rearranged formula to find $[H^+]$.*
-7.80 has 2 decimal places, so give $10^{-7.80}$ to 2 significant figures.

$$[H^+] = 10^{-7.80}$$
$$= 1.58489... \times 10^{-8}$$
$$= \textbf{1.6} \times \textbf{10}^{-8} \textbf{ mol dm}^{-3}$$

Practice Questions

Q1 The pK_a of an acid can be calculated using the expression $pK_a = -\log_{10}(K_a)$
Find the pK_a of an acid for which $K_a = 3.5 \times 10^{-8}$ mol dm^{-3}. Give your answer to 2 decimal places.

Q2 Using the formula $pH = -\log_{10} [H^+]$:

a) Find the pH of a solution of hydrochloric acid with a hydrogen ion concentration of 0.025 mol dm^{-3},

b) Find the pH of a solution of sodium hydroxide with a hydrogen ion concentration of 7.9×10^{-14} mol dm^{-3}.

c) Find the hydrogen ion concentration of a solution of ethanoic acid with a pH of 4.80.
Give your answer in standard form.

d) Find the hydrogen ion concentration of a solution of citric acid with a pH of 5.23.
Give your answer in standard form.

Q3 The expression for finding the ionic product of water, K_w, is $K_w = [H^+][OH^-]$.
At 298 K the value of K_w is 1.00×10^{-14} mol^2 dm^{-6}. Given that $pH = -\log_{10} [H^+]$, find the pH of a solution of sodium hydroxide for which $[OH^-] = 0.631$ mol dm^{-3}. Give your answer to 3 decimal places.

As easy as drumming on a dead tree trunk...

Logs can be pretty tricky, but as long as you remember the basic idea that 10^x and $\log_{10}x$ are inverses of each other (one undoes the other), you'll be fine. You might find it useful to always put the thing you're taking the log of in brackets, even if it's a single number. That way there's no chance of getting confused between, say, log (a + b) and log (a) + b.

Natural Logs

Unfortunately for you, logs with a base of ten aren't the only ones you need to know about...

Natural Logs are to Base e

The number 'e' crops up occasionally in chemistry. Like π, it's an **irrational number**, which means it has an infinite number of decimal places.

> An irrational number is one that you can't write as a fraction with whole numbers on the top and bottom. The decimal places in an irrational number go on forever and never repeat.

$$e = 2.718281828459045235360...$$

In most of the calculations involving e that you'll meet, it's raised to a **power**, so it looks like this: e^x
The function e^x is known as the 'exponential function'.

$$e^{2.00} = 7.4 \text{ (to 2 s.f.)} \qquad e^{-3.24} = 0.039 \text{ (to 2 s.f.)} \qquad e^0 = 1$$

The exponential function is a **power** with **base** e. That means all the **power laws** from page 19 apply to e^x.
It also means that there's a **logarithm** (see page 20) which is the inverse of e^x.
The log with **base e** is called the **natural logarithm**. It's usually written as **ln**.

$$\ln 7.4 = 2.00 \qquad \ln 0.039 = -3.24 \qquad \ln 1 = 0$$

Just as with base ten logs, e^x and $\ln x$ are **inverse** functions. This means that $e^{\ln x} = x$ and $\ln(e^x) = x$.
For example, $e^{\ln 2} = 2$ and $\ln(e^6) = 6$.

You Can do Calculations Involving e and ln Using Your Calculator

To raise e to a power, press: ⟹ e^x then enter the power.

This may be a 'second function' on your calculator, so you may have to press shift or second function first.

To take the natural log of a number, press: ⟹ ln   then enter the number you want the log of.

You can think of ln as an abbreviation of "log natural" if it helps you to remember the difference between log and ln.

Natural logs follow the **same rules** for significant figures and decimal places as logs with base 10 (see page 20):

1) If you take the natural log of a number, give your answer to the **same number of decimal places** as there are **significant figures** in the number. For example: $\ln 1.92 = 0.652325... = 0.652$ (to 3 d.p.).

2) If you're **raising e** to a power, give your answer to the same number of **significant figures** as there are **decimal places** in the power. For example: $e^{-6.6} = 1.360368... \times 10^{-3} = 1 \times 10^{-3}$ (to 1 s.f.).

Worked Example 1

An Arrhenius plot is a type of graph which can be used to link the temperature and activation energy of a reaction with k, the rate constant of the reaction. To draw an Arrhenius plot, values of $\ln k$ must be calculated from known values of k. The table on the right shows some values of k and $\ln k$ to be used to draw an Arrhenius plot.
Calculate the missing values A and B.

k	$\ln k$
13.0	2.565
4.51	A
0.539	−0.618
B	−1.255

1 **Use ln to find the value of A.**

4.51 has 3 significant figures, so give ln 4.51 to 3 decimal places.

$A = \ln k = \ln 4.51$
$A = 1.506$ (to 3 d.p.)

2 **Use e^x to find the value of B.**

e^x and $\ln x$ are inverses (opposites) of each other, so $k = e^{\ln k}$.
−1.255 has 3 decimal places, so give $e^{-1.255}$ to 3 significant figures.

$B = e^{\ln k} = e^{-1.255}$
$B = 0.285$ (to 3 s.f.)

Natural Logs

You Can Use **Log Rules** to Simplify Natural Log Calculations

You already know that e^x and $\ln x$ are **inverse functions** (see previous page). But there are a couple of extra **log rules** that will also come in handy when you're doing calculations with natural logs.

$$\ln (xy) = \ln (x) + \ln (y)$$

$$\ln\left(\frac{x}{y}\right) = \ln (x) - \ln (y)$$

In fact, both of these rules apply to all logs, whatever their bases are — but in chemistry you'll mostly need them for working with natural logarithms.

⟵ So you could also say, for example:
$$\log_{10}(xy) = \log_{10}(x) + \log_{10}(y)$$

Worked Example 2

The Arrhenius equation is an important equation connected to rates of reaction. It's the main place in chemistry where you might meet e and $\ln$.

The Arrhenius equation is usually written $k = Ae^{\frac{-E_a}{RT}}$.

Show that this equation can be rearranged to the form $\ln k = \ln A - \frac{E_a}{RT}$.

1 **Take the natural log of both sides of the equation.**
You'll need to get rid of that pesky e^x. You can do that by applying the inverse function, $\ln$, to both sides.

$$k = Ae^{\frac{-E_a}{RT}}$$
$$\ln k = \ln\left(Ae^{\frac{-E_a}{RT}}\right)$$

2 **Use the rule $\ln (xy) = \ln (x) + \ln (y)$.**
The right hand side is the natural log of two things multiplied together, so you can separate them out.

$$\ln\left(Ae^{\frac{-E_a}{RT}}\right) = \ln A + \ln\left(e^{\frac{-E_a}{RT}}\right)$$
$$\text{So}\quad \ln k = \ln A + \ln\left(e^{\frac{-E_a}{RT}}\right)$$

3 **Use the rule $\ln (e^x) = x$.**
Now the $\ln$ and the e cancel out to leave what was the power as a term on its own.

$$\ln k = \ln A - \frac{E_a}{RT}$$

Amy was great at simplifying logs.

Practice Questions

Use the following information to answer the questions below:

The Arrhenius equation is $k = Ae^{\frac{-E_a}{RT}}$ and its logarithmic form is $\ln k = \ln A - \frac{E_a}{RT}$,

where k = the rate constant, A = the Arrhenius constant, T = temperature in K, $R = 8.31$ J K^{-1} mol^{-1} and E_a = activation energy in J mol^{-1}.

Q1 For a certain reaction, $A = 5.02 \times 10^9$ s^{-1} and $E_a = 122\ 000$ J mol^{-1} at a temperature of 345 K.
Use the Arrhenius equation to find the value of the rate constant k at 345 K. (The units of k will be s^{-1}).

Q2 a) By rearranging the equation $\ln k = \ln A - \frac{E_a}{RT}$, show that $E_a = RT \times \ln\left(\frac{A}{k}\right)$.

b) Use the rearranged equation from part a) to find the activation energy, in joules, of a reaction where $A = 8.41 \times 10^{11}$ s^{-1} and $k = 1.83 \times 10^{-5}$ s^{-1} at a temperature of 375 K.

Q3 At temperature T, a reaction was found to have an activation energy of 367 000 J mol^{-1}.
at this temperature, the value of A was 1.21×10^{10} s^{-1}, and the value of k was 0.00710 s^{-1}.
Using the logarithmic form of the Arrhenius equation, find the value of T.

Natural logs — trees that don't wear make-up...

Natural logs and exponential functions look a bit horrid, but it's worth getting comfortable with using them. Practise taking natural logs of numbers and make sure you know how to get rid of one too. And it's definitely worth making sure you understand the second worked example — if you've got your head round what's going on there, you're laughing.

Using Units

*Whatever you're investigating in chemistry, **units** are important. Without them, a measurement just doesn't make sense. You need to be able to work out what units your answers should have..*

Here Are Some **Common Units** You Might See

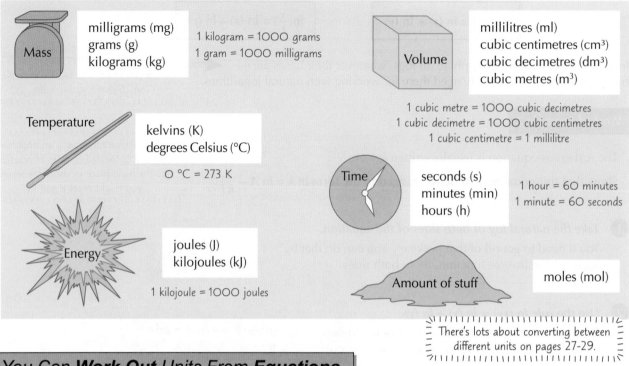

Mass — milligrams (mg), grams (g), kilograms (kg)

1 kilogram = 1000 grams
1 gram = 1000 milligrams

Volume — millilitres (ml), cubic centimetres (cm³), cubic decimetres (dm³), cubic metres (m³)

1 cubic metre = 1000 cubic decimetres
1 cubic decimetre = 1000 cubic centimetres
1 cubic centimetre = 1 millilitre

Temperature — kelvins (K), degrees Celsius (°C)

0 °C = 273 K

Time — seconds (s), minutes (min), hours (h)

1 hour = 60 minutes
1 minute = 60 seconds

Energy — joules (J), kilojoules (kJ)

1 kilojoule = 1000 joules

Amount of stuff — moles (mol)

There's lots about converting between different units on pages 27-29.

You Can **Work Out** Units From **Equations**

1) When you're doing a calculation in chemistry, you'll need to work out what **units** your answer has.

2) If you're using a **formula** that **only** contains **additions** and **subtractions**, then the units of the answer will be the **same** as the units of the values in your equation. For example:

> A student measured the temperature of a solution before and after a reaction took place.
> She measured the **initial temperature** of the solution as **293 K** and its **final temperature** as **318 K**.
> What was the temperature change of the solution?
>
> Temperature change = final temperature – initial temperature
> = 318 K – 293 K = **25 K**

3) If you're using a more complicated formula that contains **multiplications** and **division**, all you need to do to find the units of the answer is to pop the units that you already know into the **same formula**. For example:

> A student made up a solution of sodium chloride by dissolving **0.25 moles** of table salt in **0.5 dm³** of water. What was the **concentration** of the solution he made?
>
> $$\text{concentration} = \frac{\text{number of moles}}{\text{volume}} = 0.25 \div 0.5 = \textbf{0.5}$$
>
> $$\text{units of concentration} = \frac{\text{units of number of moles}}{\text{units of volume}} = \frac{\text{mol}}{\text{dm}^3} = \textbf{mol dm}^{-3}$$
>
> Concentration of solution = **0.5 mol dm⁻³**

Any unit like this that's made up of a combination of one unit multiplied or divided by another is called a compound unit.

- When you have a unit involving a fraction (or a division) like this one, any positive powers on the bottom of the fraction (or that you are dividing by) become negative and any negative powers become positive.
- This works because of the power law $\frac{1}{a^n} = a^{-n}$ (see page 18).
- You could add an extra step to the units calculation and write it as $\frac{\text{mol}}{\text{dm}^3} = \text{mol} \times \frac{1}{\text{dm}^3} = \text{mol dm}^{-3}$ — this make it easier to see where the 'dm⁻³' bit comes from.

Using Units

Worked Example 1

A reaction mixture produces 12 cm^3 of carbon dioxide gas in 24 seconds.
Using the equation 'rate = amount of product formed ÷ time', find the rate of the reaction, including its units.

1 **Put the numbers into the equation to find the rate.**

The amount of product formed is 12 cm^3 and the time is 24 seconds.　　$12 ÷ 24 = 0.5$

2 **Put the units into the equation to find the units of the rate.**

The units for the amount of product formed are cm^3
and the units of time are seconds.　　$cm^3 ÷ s = \text{units of rate}$

3 **Get rid of the ÷ sign.**

Make positive powers of any units you're dividing by negative, and negative
powers of any units you're dividing by positive. So '÷ s' becomes 's^{-1}'.　　$cm^3 ÷ s = cm^3\ s^{-1}$

4 **Combine the numerical answer with the units to give your final answer.**

The rate is **0.5 cm^3 s^{-1}**

> Rate can be measured in lots of different units, e.g. dm^3 min^{-1}, mol s^{-1}, so it's particularly important to include units when your answer is a rate.

For Some Quantities, You'll Have to **Work Out** the Units **Every Time**

1) Some quantities, such as **equilibrium constants** and **rate constants** have **variable units**.
2) This is because the **expressions** for these quantities change depending on the **reaction** you're looking at.
3) This means you have to work out the units for these quantities separately each time you do a calculation.
4) The steps are the same as the ones on the previous page, except that you should start by writing out an **expression** for the constant you're finding.

Worked Example 2

Find the units for the equilibrium constant, K_c, given that $K_c = \dfrac{[B][C]}{[A]^2}$.
([X] = concentration of X in mol dm^{-3}.)

1 **Write out the expression for the equilibrium constant.**　　$K_c = \dfrac{[B][C]}{[A]^2}$

2 **Put the units into the expression.**
All the concentrations are in mol dm^{-3}.

$$\text{units of } K_c = \frac{(mol\ dm^{-3})(mol\ dm^{-3})}{(mol\ dm^{-3})^2} = \frac{(mol\ dm^{-3})(mol\ dm^{-3})}{(mol\ dm^{-3})(mol\ dm^{-3})}$$

3 **Cancel out units that are on the top and the bottom of the fraction.**

if the same unit is present on both the top and the
bottom of a fraction, you can cancel them out.

Here, the two 'mol dm^{-3}' terms on top of the fraction
will cancel with the ones on the bottom of the fraction:

$$\text{units of } K_c = \frac{\cancel{(mol\ dm^{-3})}\cancel{(mol\ dm^{-3})}}{\cancel{(mol\ dm^{-3})}\cancel{(mol\ dm^{-3})}} = \frac{1}{1}$$

4 **If all the units cancel, the constant has no units.**　　$\text{units of } K_c = $ **no units**

Using Units

The rate equation for a reaction is given by the expression rate = $k[A]$. [A] is the concentration of A given in mol dm^{-3}, and the rate of the reaction is given in mol dm^{-3} s^{-1}.

What are the units of the rate constant, k?

The units of cuteness are 'aww's.

1 **Rearrange the rate equation to find an expression for the rate constant.**

The rate equation is rate = $k[A]$, which rearranges to give:

$$k = \frac{rate}{[A]}$$

There's loads more about rearranging equations on pages 42-45.

2 **Put the units into the expression.**

The concentration of A is in mol dm^{-3} and the rate is in mol dm^{-3} s^{-1}.

$$\text{units of } k = \frac{\text{mol dm}^{-3}\text{ s}^{-1}}{\text{mol dm}^{-3}}$$

3 **Cancel out any units that are on the top and the bottom of the fraction.**

The 'mol dm^{-3}' part of the rate units on top of the fraction will cancel with the 'mol dm^{-3}' on the bottom of the fraction:

$$\text{units of } k = \frac{\cancel{\text{mol dm}^{-3}}\text{ s}^{-1}}{\cancel{\text{mol dm}^{-3}}} = \frac{\text{s}^{-1}}{1}$$

4 **If all the units on the bottom of the fraction cancel, the units of the rate constant are just what's left on the top of the fraction.**

units of k = s^{-1}

Practice Questions

Q1   A student dissolved 0.35 g of hydrated copper sulfate in 0.07 dm^3 of water. Calculate the concentration of the solution, including units, using the equation *concentration = mass ÷ volume*.

Q2   During a reaction, the mass of the reaction vessel decreases by 15 g over 6.0 minutes as a gas is formed and lost from the mixture. Find the rate of the reaction, including units, using the equation *rate = amount of product formed ÷ time*.

Q3   The gas equilibrium constant, K_p for the reaction $2NO_2 \rightleftharpoons N_2O_4$ is given by the expression:

$K_p = \dfrac{p_{N_2O_4}}{(p_{NO_2})^2}$, where p_X is the partial pressure of X in kPa.

What are the units of the gas equilibrium constant for this reaction?

K_p is just like K_c, except that each component is given as a partial pressure rather than a concentration.

Q4   Find the units of the rate constant, k, in each of the following rate equations, given that the units of rate are mol dm^{-3} s^{-1}, and the concentrations of all the substances are given in mol dm^{-3}.

    a)   rate = $k[NO]^2$

    b)   rate = $k[C(CH_3)_3I]$

    c)   rate = $k[NO]^2[H_2]$

Hint: All of the power laws covered on pages 18-19 apply to units too. E.g. mol × mol = mol^2, dm^{-3} × dm^{-3} = dm$^{-3 + -3}$ = dm^{-6}.

You knit, Zainab crochets and I make tiny patchwork elephants...

It can help to write down the units next to each value in a calculation so you don't get in a pickle. This also means you can easily check whether your answer has the right units. Working out units when fractions are involved can seem a bit strange and complicated to begin with, so have another look at the worked examples to make sure you've really got it.

Converting Units

You often need to convert quantities into different units for equations, or just to make them easier to handle.

Quantities in Chemistry come in a **Huge Range** of Sizes

Volume of a
carbon atom
$\approx 9.97 \times 10^{-30}$ m³

 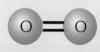
Mass of a
hydrogen atom
$\approx 1.66 \times 10^{-24}$ g

 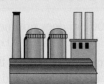
Energy needed to break
one O=O double bond
$\approx 8.27 \times 10^{-19}$ J

Volume of
1 mole of a gas
under standard
conditions
$\approx 2.40 \times 10^{-2}$ m³

Energy produced
by burning 1 mol
of propane
$\approx 2.22 \times 10^{6}$ J

Pressure used in
a chemical plant
producing ammonia
$\approx 2.0 \times 10^{7}$ Pa

1) The quantities shown above are given in **basic units** (like **grams** and **joules**).

2) There are **prefixes** you can put in front of these units to make the name of a **larger** or **smaller** unit.

3) Here are the main ones you'll need to use at A-level:

prefix	kilo (k)	none	deci (d)	centi (c)	milli (m)
multiple of unit	1000	1	0.1	0.01	0.001

4) These prefixes tell you that a unit is **ten**, a **hundred** or a **thousand** times bigger or smaller than the basic unit. For example, one kilogram is one thousand grams (1 kg = 1000 g) and one centimetre is one hundredth of a metre (1 cm³ = 0.01 m).

Watch out for units of volume though — they're a bit tricky. There's more on this on the next page.

You Can **Convert** From One Unit to Another

1) Knowing how different units are related to each other will help you swap from one unit to another.

2) All you need to know is what number you have to divide or multiply by to get from the original unit to the new unit — this is called the **conversion factor**.

3) To go from a **bigger** unit (like m) to a **smaller** unit (like cm), you **multiply** by the conversion factor. To go from a **smaller** unit (like g) to a **bigger** unit (like kg), you **divide** by the conversion factor.

Here are the most common unit conversions that you'll need to do:

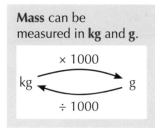
Mass can be measured in **kg** and **g**.

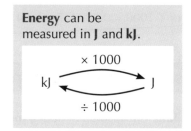
Energy can be measured in **J** and **kJ**.

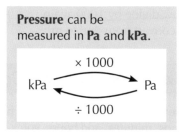
Pressure can be measured in **Pa** and **kPa**.

It's easy to get muddled when you're converting between units, but there's a general rule to check your answer:

- If you're moving from a **smaller unit** to a **larger unit** (e.g. g to kg) then the number should get **smaller**.
- If you're moving from a **larger unit** to a **smaller unit** (e.g. cm to mm) then the number should get **bigger**.

Worked Example 1

Convert 1427 Pa into kPa.

You're moving to a larger unit, and the number has become smaller, so this looks right.

1 **Divide by 1000.**

Using the conversions above, divide by 1000 to go from Pa to kPa: 1427 Pa ÷ 1000 = **1.427 kPa**

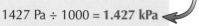

Converting Units

Convert 0.142 kilojoules into joules.

1 *Multiply by 1000.*

From the previous page, you multiply by 1000 to convert from kJ to J, so:

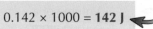

$$0.142 \times 1000 = \mathbf{142\ J}$$

You're moving to a smaller unit, and the number has become larger, so this looks right.

Volumes and *Areas* are a Bit More *Tricky*

Just because 1 m = 100 cm **does not** mean that 1 m³ = 100 cm³.
In fact, $1\ m^3 = 1\ m \times 1\ m \times 1\ m = 100\ cm \times 100\ cm \times 100\ cm$, so $\mathbf{1\ m^3 = 1\ 000\ 000\ cm^3}$.

If a measurement is **squared** or **cubed**, then you need to do the **same thing** to the conversion factor. This generally comes up with areas and volumes:

> 1) The units of area are **squared**, so **square** the scaling factor.
> 2) The units of a volume are **cubed**, so **cube** the scaling factor.

Here are the most common conversions you'll need to do for units of volume:

To convert from m to dm, you'd divide by 10. So to convert from m³ to dm³, divide by 10³ = 1000.

Volume can be measured in **m³**, **dm³** and **cm³**.

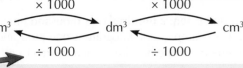

Convert 437 cm³ into m³.

1 *Convert cm³ to dm³.*

First convert from cm³ to dm³ by dividing by 1000:

$$437\ cm^3 \div 1000 = 0.437\ dm^3$$

If you remembered that 1 m³ = 1 000 000 cm³, you could convert from cm³ to m³ in one step by dividing by 1 000 000.

2 *Convert dm³ to m³.*

Now divide by 1000 again to convert from dm³ to m³:

$$0.437\ dm^3 \div 1000 = 0.000437\ m^3 = \mathbf{4.37 \times 10^{-4}\ m^3}$$

Time and *Temperature* Conversions Are a Bit *Different*

To convert between units of time, such as seconds, minutes, and hours, you can't just divide by a multiple of ten:

For example, 1.25 min is not the same as 1 minute and 25 seconds. (0.25 × 60) = 15, so it's 1 minute and 15 seconds.

Time is measured in **hours**, **min** and **s**.

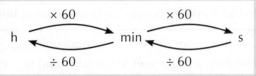

To convert between degrees celsius and kelvins, you **add** or **subtract** 273:

Temperature can be measured in **K** and **°C**.

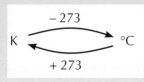

Converting Units

Units in *Calculations* Should *Match*

1) All quantities of the **same type** in one calculation should have the **same unit**. So, for example, if you have two different volumes in your calculation, the units of both must be the same.

2) This is the case even if the units are within **compound units**.
So, for example, if you have a volume and a rate in your calculation, and the volume is in units of cm^3, the rate must be in units of units of $cm^3\ s^{-1}$ (not, for example, $dm^3\ s^{-1}$).

3) Before you do a calculation, you need to make sure that all the same **types** of quantities have the same **units**. If they don't, you'll have to **convert** your units first, so they are all the same, and then do the calculation.

Worked Example 4

The enthalpy change of a reaction is $-206\ kJ\ mol^{-1}$ and the entropy change is $80.0\ J\ mol^{-1}\ K^{-1}$.
Calculate the free energy change at 325 K using the equation $\Delta G = \Delta H - T\Delta S$.
ΔG is the free energy change, ΔH is the enthalpy change, ΔS is the entropy change and T is the temperature.

1 *Check that units of the same type are the same.*
Units of temperature = K. Units of entropy change = $J\ mol^{-1}\ K^{-1}$.
- Both temperature units are in K, so neither needs to be converted.

It doesn't matter if the same unit is raised to different powers, like the 'K's here — you can use the power laws to sort the powers out when you do the calculation.

Units of enthalpy change = $kJ\ mol^{-1}$. Units of entropy change = $J\ mol^{-1}\ K^{-1}$.
- Both amount of substance units are in mol, so neither needs to be converted.
- There's a mixture of kJ and J in the energy units — you need to convert one of them so that they match.

2 *Convert the enthalpy into $J\ mol^{-1}$.*
$1\ kJ = 1000\ J$, so $1\ kJ\ mol^{-1} = 1000\ J\ mol^{-1}$

$-206\ kJ\ mol^{-1} \times 1000 = -206\ 000\ J\ mol^{-1}$

You could convert the entropy change to $kJ\ mol^{-1}\ K^{-1}$ instead.

3 *Plug all your numbers into the equation, and do the calculation.*
$\Delta H = -206\ 000\ J\ mol^{-1}$, $\Delta S = 80.0\ J\ mol^{-1}\ K^{-1}$,
$T = 325\ K$

$\Delta G = \Delta H - T\Delta S$
$\Delta G = -206\ 000\ J\ mol^{-1} - (325\ K \times 80.0\ J\ mol^{-1}\ K^{-1})$
$= -206\ 000\ J\ mol^{-1} - 26\ 000\ J\ mol^{-1}$
$= -232\ 000\ J\ mol^{-1}$

$K \times K^{-1} = 1$, so the temperature units cancel out.

Worked Example 5

During a reaction, it took 2 minutes for 0.60 mol of product to form.
Find the rate of the reaction in $mol\ s^{-1}$.

1 *Convert the time from minutes to seconds.*
The question asks for units in $mol\ s^{-1}$. So before you start the calculation, you should convert the units of time from min to s.

$2\ min \times 60 = 120\ s$

2 *Calculate the rate.*
Rate = amount of product formed ÷ time, so: rate $= 0.60\ mol \div 120 = 0.005\ mol\ s^{-1} = 5 \times 10^{-3}\ mol\ s^{-1}$

Practice Questions

Q1 Convert the following:
a) 240 g to kilograms.   b) $4.1\ kJ\ mol^{-1}$ to joules per mole.   c) $0.5\ dm^3$ to cubic centimetres.

Q2 A reaction takes 4.6 minutes to go to completion. How many seconds is this?

Q3 During a titration, $31\ cm^3$ of an alkali is needed to neutralise $0.025\ dm^3$ of an acid.
What is the total volume of the acid and the alkali in cm^3?

My pet snake has a scale factor of 1×10^3...

Always double check the numbers when you're converting between units. If you're going from small units to larger units, the number should get smaller, and if you're going from large units to smaller units, the number should get bigger.

Tables of Data

OK, I'll admit it, this topic is pretty simple stuff — you've probably been making and using data tables for as long as you can remember. But, though it's simple maths, you'll be using tables all the time in chemistry — so it's worth a quick recap.

Tables Show Data in Rows and Columns

In Chemistry, tables are used to **present data** and **record the results** from your experiments.

Here's an example of a simple results table:

Temperature of reaction mixture (°C)	Initial Rate (mol dm^{-3} s^{-1})
15	1.2×10^{-3}
20	2.5×10^{-3}
25	3.6×10^{-3}
30	4.5×10^{-3}
35	5.6×10^{-3}

The **top row** has headings showing what's recorded in each column.

In this table, each row tells you what the **initial rate** of the experiment was at a **certain temperature**.

For example, this row tells you that when the experiment was run at 35 °C, it had an initial rate of 5.6×10^{-3} mol dm^{-3} s^{-1}.

Here's a more complicated results table — this one shows the results for several **repeats** of an experiment:

Concentration of HCl / mol dm^{-3}	Time taken for mark to be obscured / s				Mean time taken for mark to be obscured / s
	Run 1	Run 2	Run 3	Run 4	
0.10	58	57	60	57	58
0.20	30	30	32	32	31
0.30	12	16	17	15	15

Showing the results for all the repeats of an experiment helps you to spot if there are any **anomalous results** (see page 32) and to look for patterns in your data.

You can read the column and row labels to work out what a number means. For example, this tells you that, in the second run of the experiment, it took 16 seconds for the mark to be obscured when 0.30 mol dm^{-3} hydrochloric acid was used.

Results tables often have an extra column for recording the **mean** (average) result. For more about finding means, see pages 32-33.

Be Careful with Units in Tables

Reading information from a table should be pretty straightforward. All you do is...

1) Find the **row** or **column heading** that corresponds to the piece of data that you need to know.

2) Read **down** or **across** from the relevant heading to find the entry you're looking for, paying attention to the **units**.

Nick got the wrong idea when he was asked to make a table.

Remember, if you have to **draw** a table...

1) Include a **clear heading** for each row and column.

2) Include the **units** in the **headings** for any data that needs them. Make sure all the information in a row or column is in the same units.

Time (s)	Concentration of NaOH (mol dm^{-3})
0	1.00
20	0.88
40	0.80
60	0.76

Some tables show the units in brackets like this one, others use a slash (e.g. time / s). Don't worry though — as long as it's clear what you mean, you can use any format for the units.

Tables of Data

Worked Example

A student measured out 10 cm³ samples of three different concentrations of hydrochloric acid. He added each one to a test tube containing 5 g of calcium carbonate. He measured the volume of carbon dioxide gas that had been produced by each tube after 30 s, 60 s and 90 s.

His results are shown in the table on the right.

Concentration of acid / mol dm⁻³	Volume of gas collected (cm³)		
	After 30 s	After 60 s	After 90 s
0.40	7.5	14.0	19.5
0.60	10.5	21.5	29.5
1.0	19.5	35.0	42.5

What volume of gas had the student collected from the test tube containing 1 mol dm⁻³ acid after 60 s?

1 *Find the row showing the results for the runs when the student used 1.0 mol dm⁻³ acid.*

Concentration of acid / mol dm⁻³	Volume of gas collected (cm³)		
	After 30 s	After 60 s	After 90 s
0.40	7.5	14.0	19.5
0.60	10.5	21.5	29.5
1.0	19.5	35.0	42.5

This row shows the volume of gas collected at all three time points when the student was using 1.0 mol dm⁻³ acid.

2 *Read across the row until you reach the column showing the volume of gas collected after 60 s.*

Concentration of acid / mol dm⁻³	Volume of gas collected (cm³)		
	After 30 s	After 60 s	After 90 s
0.40	7.5	14.0	19.5
0.60	10.5	21.5	29.5
1.0	19.5	35.0	42.5

This column shows the volume of gas collected after 60 s in each experiment.

The volume of gas collected by the student after 60 s when he was using 1.0 mol dm⁻³ acid is the value where the column and row meet.

When the student was using 1.0 mol dm⁻³ acid, he had collected **35.0 cm³** of gas after 60 s.

Practice Question

Q1 A student was given a sample of sulfuric acid (H_2SO_4) of unknown concentration. She titrated the acid with two different concentrations of NaOH solution. Her results are shown in the table below. Use the table to answer the following questions

a) What volume of 0.1 mol dm⁻³ NaOH did the student add during run 1?

b) In which run of the experiment did the student add 38.00 cm³ of 0.3 mol dm⁻³ NaOH to the acid?

c) What was the smallest volume of NaOH that the student added in any single run of the experiment?

d) What total volume of 0.3 mol dm⁻³ NaOH did the student use across all three runs?

Concentration of NaOH / mol dm⁻³	Volume of NaOH needed to neutralise the acid / cm³		
	Run 1	Run 2	Run 3
0.1	12.50	12.75	12.25
0.3	36.75	38.00	37.75

I used to be terrible at recording data — but now the tables have turned...

You'll have to be able draw clear, sensible tables of results for any chemistry experiments that you do, as well as being able to read information accurately from tables that other people have made. Make sure that you've got both of these skills mastered. And remember, always check what the units in the headings are before you do anything with the data.

Finding the Mean

*When you're collecting data from an experiment, you'll normally repeat each measurement at least three times. Then you'll need to calculate a **mean**...*

You Should Calculate a Mean of **Repeated Measurements**

If you repeatedly measured how long it took to boil a beaker of water from room temperature, you'd get a slightly different result each time:

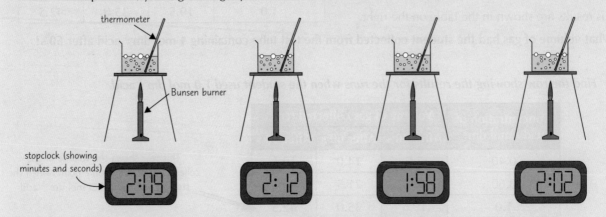

thermometer

Bunsen burner

stopclock (showing minutes and seconds)

2:09   2:12   1:58   2:02

This is because, even if you're careful, there will be **small variations** in the experiment between each repeat that are **outside your control** (e.g. impurities in the water) that affect how long the water takes to boil.

Taking an **average** of repeated measurements **cancels out** some of this variation, and can help you get an answer that's closer to the true value you're interested in.

The average you need to know about in chemistry is the **mean**.

There's a **Simple Formula** for Calculating the Mean

You'll have come across the formula for the mean before:

$$\text{mean (average)} = \frac{\text{sum of your repeated measurements}}{\text{number of repeats taken}}$$

People told Gerald that he was especially mean, but he thought he was only averagely so.

For the example above, you'd convert the times into seconds first (so the measurements are in one unit), and then:

$$\text{mean} = \frac{129 + 132 + 118 + 122}{4} = 125.25 \text{ s} = \textbf{125 seconds (to 3 s.f.)}$$

If you wanted to, you could convert this back to **2 minutes 5 seconds (to the nearest second)**.

Anomalous Results Shouldn't be Included in Mean Calculations

1) An **anomalous result** is just any result that doesn't fit the pattern of the rest of the data.

2) Anomalous results are usually caused by **experimental errors** or **human error**.

3) Anomalous results would make the value of the mean **higher** or **lower** than it should be (this is sometimes called skewing the value of the mean). So you need to identify them and **leave them out** when you're finding the mean.

Concentration of NaOH / mol dm^{-3}	Rate of reaction / mol dm^{-3} s^{-1}			
	Run 1	Run 2	Run 3	Run 4
0.2	0.010	0.012	0.011	0.043
0.4	0.022	0.025	0.023	0.021

For example, if you were asked to calculate the mean rate of reaction for 0.2 mol dm^{-3} NaOH here, you should ignore the result for run 4 — it doesn't fit in with the other results for that concentration.

Finding the Mean

Worked Example

The table below shows the results of five repeated measurements of the volume of 0.5 mol dm⁻³
HCl that was required to neutralise 50 cm³ of a solution of KOH of unknown concentration.
During one of the repeats, a problem with the burette caused the volume of acid needed to
neutralise the alkali to be measured incorrectly.

Repeat	1	2	3	4	5
Volume of HCl / cm³	25.05	25.00	27.50	25.10	25.05

a) State which result was measured incorrectly.

b) Calculate the mean volume of HCl needed to neutralise 50 cm³ of the KOH solution.

1 *Identify the anomalous result.*

Apart from repeat 3, all of the values for volume are between 25.00 cm³ and 25.10 cm³.
The result for repeat 3 is at least 2.4 cm³ higher than all the other results.

The result for **repeat 3** was recorded incorrectly.

2 *Add up the rest of the volumes,
then divide by the number of repeats.*

Remember, since you're not including
repeat 3, the number of repeats is 4, not 5.

$$\text{mean volume} = \frac{25.05 + 25.00 + 25.10 + 25.05}{4} = \textbf{25.05 cm}^3$$

Practice Questions

Q1 A experiment to measure the yield of a chemical reaction was repeated three times.
The first time the yield was found to be 15.7 g, the second time 16.5 g and the third time 16.0 g.

Calculate the mean yield of the reaction.

Q2 A student used a calorimeter to measure the heat energy given out by a reaction.
She then used this measurement to calculate the enthalpy change of the reaction in kJ mol⁻¹.
She repeated this process five times. Her final results are shown in the table below.

Repeat	1	2	3	4	5
Enthalpy change of reaction / kJ mol⁻¹	−2866	−2879	−2876	−1869	−2888

a) For one of the repeats, the calorimeter was not completely sealed and heat was lost to the surroundings.
Suggest which repeat this error has affected.

b) Calculate the mean enthalpy change of the reaction, ignoring the anomalous result.

Q3 A student was given a solution of nitric
acid (HNO₃) of unknown concentration.
He titrated the acid with two different
concentrations of sodium hydroxide (NaOH).
His results are shown in the table on the right.

a) Find the mean volume of 0.02 mol dm⁻³
NaOH needed to neutralise the acid.

Concentration of NaOH / mol dm⁻³	Volume of NaOH needed to neutralise the acid / cm³			
	Run 1	Run 2	Run 3	Run 4
0.02	55.40	55.40	55.50	55.50
0.04	27.20	27.25	19.00	27.15

b) Find the mean volume of 0.04 mol dm⁻³ NaOH needed to neutralise the acid, ignoring anomalous results.

c) For part b), describe what effect it would have on the mean if you included the anomalous result(s).

I must admit, making you learn these pages is pretty mean...

*Hopefully you'll have come across most of this stuff already — just make sure when you're looking at a set of data
that you identify the anomalies and don't include them when calculating a mean. Otherwise you might end up with a
skewed mean, and nobody wants that. I had a friend who skewed his mean once — took him weeks to get over it.*

The Mean and Relative Atomic Mass

*"What has finding the **relative atomic mass** of an element got to do with handling data?" I hear you cry (not unreasonably). Well, relative atomic mass is really just a special type of mean, calculated from data about an element's isotopes.*

Relative Atomic Mass is the Mean Mass of One Atom of an Element

The **relative atomic mass** (A_r) of an element is the **mean mass** of **one atom** of that element, on a scale where the mass of one atom of carbon-12 is exactly 12.

If you look at the periodic table, you'll see that for most elements A_r **isn't** a whole number. This is because the A_r takes into account the **relative masses** of the different **isotopes** of an element (often called their **relative isotopic masses**).

> 28.1
> **Si**
> silicon
> 14

Isotopes of an element are atoms with the same number of protons but different numbers of neutrons.

For example, **silicon** has three commonly occurring isotopes: silicon-28, silicon-29 and silicon-30. So its relative atomic mass takes into account the relative mass of each isotope.

But relative atomic mass **isn't** a simple mean — you can't find the A_r of silicon by adding up the relative masses of the three isotopes and dividing by three. You need to take into account the **abundance** of each isotope too.

	Natural abundance (%)
Silicon-28	92.23
Silicon-29	4.67
Silicon-30	3.10

If you look at the table on the left you'll see that most silicon atoms are silicon-28 — any single atom of silicon you find is **far more likely** to have a relative mass of 28 than 29 or 30.

So to find the mean mass of **every single atom of silicon** (A_r), you have to **multiply** the relative mass of each isotope by its **abundance** and **divide** by the **sum of the abundances**.

$$A_r \text{ of silicon} = \frac{(92.23 \times 28) + (4.67 \times 29) + (3.10 \times 30)}{92.23 + 4.67 + 3.10} = 2810.87 \div 100 = 28.1087 = \textbf{28.1 (3 s.f.)}$$

A mean like this that takes into account the **"importance"** of each value is called a **weighted mean**.

Use Relative Isotopic Mass And Abundance to Find Relative Atomic Mass

To find the **relative atomic mass** of an element, you need to know both the **relative isotopic mass** and the **abundance** of each of its commonly occurring **isotopes**.

If you've got the abundance of the different isotopes as **percentages**, the sum of the abundances will **always** add up to **100**.

So all you need to do to find the relative atomic mass is:

1) Multiply each relative isotopic mass by its % isotopic abundance.
2) Add up the results.
3) Divide by 100.

Steven had a large mass, relatively.

Worked Example 1

75.0% of chlorine atoms have a relative isotopic mass of 35.0, while 25.0% have a relative isotopic mass of 37.0. **Calculate the relative atomic mass of chlorine.**

1 *Multiply each relative isotopic mass by its % abundance.* $(75.0 \times 35) = \textbf{2625}$ $(25.0 \times 37.0) = \textbf{925}$

2 *Add up the results.* $2625 + 925 = \textbf{3550}$

3 *Divide by 100.*   relative atomic mass of chlorine = $3550 \div 100 = \textbf{35.5}$

The Mean and Relative Atomic Mass

Worked Example 2

Sulfur has four stable isotopes; ^{32}S, ^{33}S, ^{34}S and ^{36}S. The percentage abundances of these isotopes are: ^{32}S = 95.0%, ^{33}S = 0.750%, ^{34}S = 4.21%, ^{36}S = 0.0200%.
Calculate the relative atomic mass of sulfur.

^{32}S is just a different way of writing sulfur-32.

1 *Multiply each relative isotopic mass by its % abundance.*

$(95.0 \times 32) = \textbf{3040}$ $(0.750 \times 33) = \textbf{24.75}$ $(4.21 \times 34) = \textbf{143.14}$ $(0.0200 \times 36) = \textbf{0.72}$

2 *Add up the results.* $3040 + 24.75 + 143.14 + 0.72 = \textbf{3208.61}$

3 *Divide by 100.*   relative atomic mass of sulfur = $3208.61 \div 100 = 32.0861 = $ **32.1 (to 3 s.f.)**

If you're given the abundance of the different isotopes as **relative abundances** rather than percentages, the abundances **won't** add up to 100 — so you need a slightly different method:

1) Multiply each relative isotopic mass by its relative abundance.
2) Add up the results.
3) Divide by the **sum of the relative abundances**.

Worked Example 3

Magnesium has three stable isotopes; ^{24}Mg, ^{25}Mg and ^{26}Mg.
The relative abundances of these isotopes are: ^{24}Mg = 158, ^{25}Mg = 20.0, ^{26}Mg = 22.0
Calculate the relative atomic mass of magnesium.

1 *Multiply each relative isotopic mass by its relative abundance.*

$(158 \times 24) = \textbf{3792}$ $(20.0 \times 25) = \textbf{500}$ $(22.0 \times 26) = \textbf{572}$

2 *Add up the results.* $3792 + 500 + 572 = \textbf{4864}$

3 *Divide by the sum of the relative abundances.*   relative atomic mass of magnesium = $4864 \div (158 + 20 + 22) = 4864 \div 200$
$= 24.32 = $ **24.3 (to 3 s.f.)**

Practice Questions

Q1 Boron has two stable isotopes. 20.0% of boron atoms have a relative isotopic mass of 10.0, while 80.0% have a relative isotopic mass of 11.0. Calculate the relative atomic mass of boron.

Q2 Carbon has a relative atomic mass of 12.011. A student states that carbon only has one isotope. Is the student correct? Explain your answer.

Q3 Rubidium has two isotopes, ^{85}Rb and ^{87}Rb. Use the relative abundances shown in the table on the right to calculate the relative atomic mass of rubidium.

	Relative abundances
Rubidium-85	180.5
Rubidium-87	67.5

I think this isotopic topic is too tiresome to pick up...

...try saying that three times fast. If only all the atoms of an element had the same number of neutrons, you wouldn't have to learn about this relative atomic mass business. Alas, the universe didn't work out that way and you do need to know it. It's a cruel world. But on the bright side, there's ice cream, sunshine, kittens and monster trucks — so it's not all bad.

Uncertainty and Error

*As with all things in life, when you are measuring something, there'll always be some amount of **uncertainty**.*

All Measurements Have Some Uncertainty

Imagine you're measuring the amount of NaOH solution remaining in a burette and recording the volume to the nearest 0.1 cm³.

You might be able to take measurements more accurately than this using some burettes, but the principle will be the same.

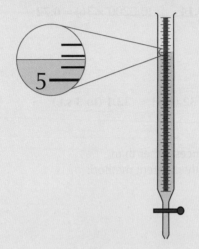

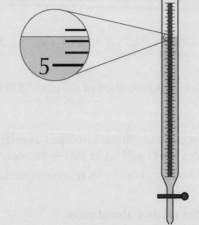

Pickles was fairly certain that he'd measured his shoe size incorrectly.

Here the volume of the solution is **between 5.1 cm³ and 5.2 cm³**.

It's **closer** to **5.2 cm³**, so you'd record its volume as **5.2 cm³**.

Here the volume of the solution is between **5.2 cm³** and **5.3 cm³**.

Again, it's **closer** to **5.2 cm³**, so that's what you'd record.

If someone else read your measurement of 10.2 cm³ in a results table, they **wouldn't know** whether the volume was actually **a little bit less** than 10.2 cm³, or a **little bit more**.

So there is some **uncertainty** in the measurement.

Uncertainties give you the **range** in which the true value of a measurement lies.

You Can Find the Uncertainty from the Scale on Your Equipment

1) If you need to, you can work out uncertainty in your measurement from the scale on your equipment:

> The uncertainty is generally **half the smallest division** the equipment can measure, in **either direction**.

2) For example, the burette in the example above has markings **every 0.1 cm³**, so 0.1 cm³ is the smallest division it can measure. The uncertainty in any measurement made with this burette is 0.1 ÷ 2 = **0.05 cm³** either way.

3) So the volume reading from the burette example above, given with the uncertainty in its measurement, is:

> **volume = 5.2 ±0.05 cm³**

The maximum possible difference between your measured value and the true value (±0.05 cm³ here) is sometimes called the 'margin of error'.

4) The sign ± means '**plus or minus**'. So the real volume here could be anywhere between 5.2 − 0.05 = **5.15 cm³** and 5.2 + 0.05 = **5.25 cm³**.

5) Sometimes, pieces of equipment will tell you the uncertainty in their measurements. For example a piece of glassware, like a volumetric flask, may have ±0.1 cm³ written on its side.

You may also see the uncertainty of a piece of equipment being called the 'error' on that equipment.

Uncertainty and Error

You Can Give Uncertainties as **Percentages**

1) Imagine you've got a balance that measures mass with an uncertainty of ±0.1 g

> If you measure a mass of **60 g**, the uncertainty is **quite small** compared to the size of the measurement.
> If you measure a mass of **0.4 g**, then the uncertainty is **nearly as big** as the measurement itself.

2) You can turn uncertainties into **percentages** to show how the size of the uncertainty compares to the size of the measurement.

3) To turn an **uncertainty** into a **percentage uncertainty**:

$$\text{percentage uncertainty} = \frac{\text{uncertainty}}{\text{reading}} \times 100$$

> The terms 'percentage uncertainty' and 'percentage error' are often used interchangeably, so you may get asked to calculate the percentage error — don't worry it's the same thing.

Worked Example

The EMF of an electrochemical cell is measured as 0.86 V.
The voltmeter has an error of ±0.02 V.
Calculate the percentage uncertainty in the EMF value.

1 *Divide the uncertainty by the reading.* $0.02 \div 0.86 = \mathbf{0.023}$

2 *Multiply the result by 100 to get a percentage.* $0.023 \times 100 = 2.3\%$
Percentage uncertainty = **±2.3%** ← So you could write the EMF as EMF = 0.86 V ±2.3%

4) If you ever need to turn a percentage uncertainty back into an uncertainty, you can just do the opposite — **divide by 100** and then **multiply by the reading** to find the uncertainty on the equipment.

5) The **larger the reading** you take with a piece of apparatus, the **smaller the percentage uncertainty** will be. This means you can **reduce** percentage uncertainty in your experiments by planning to take **larger readings**.

Practice Questions

Q1 A measuring cylinder has markings every 1 cm³.
What is the uncertainty in a measurement taken using this measuring cylinder?

Q2 During an experiment, a balance with an uncertainty of ±0.01 g was used to weigh out 0.25 g of a compound.
   a) Calculate the percentage uncertainty on this measurement.
   b) Another student plans to repeat the experiment using the same balance.
      Suggest what this student could do to reduce the percentage uncertainty in the measurement.

Q3 A student uses a voltmeter to measure the potential difference of an electrochemical cell.
In their write-up, they record their measurement as 0.41 V ±5%.
What is the uncertainty in volts of a measurement taken using this voltmeter?

Q4 A student is trying to decide which of two volumetric flasks to use in an experiment.
Flask A has an uncertainty of ±1% and flask B has an uncertainty of ±0.1 cm³.
The student needs to make 150 cm³ of a solution.
Which volumetric flask should she use to minimise the uncertainty in her measurement?

My feelings on learning about uncertainty = Unhappy ±0%...

This stuff is really important in Chemistry as it helps you to judge the validity of your results. If you learn the rules for finding uncertainties in measurements, and how to convert them to percentage uncertainties, you're on to a winner.

Combining Uncertainties

If you need to combine measurements in some way while you're working with them, you'll also need to be able to combine the uncertainties in your measurements too.

Sometimes You Need to **Combine Uncertainties**

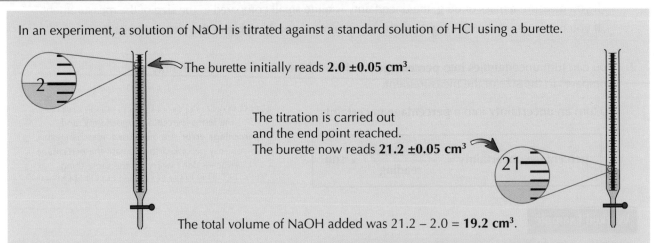

In an experiment, a solution of NaOH is titrated against a standard solution of HCl using a burette.

The burette initially reads **2.0 ±0.05 cm³**.

The titration is carried out and the end point reached. The burette now reads **21.2 ±0.05 cm³**

The total volume of NaOH added was 21.2 – 2.0 = **19.2 cm³**.

There are **two sources** of **uncertainty** in this value — the **initial burette reading** and the **final burette reading**. You need to know how to **combine** the two to find the uncertainty in the overall measurement.

If You **Combine Measurements**, You Should **Combine Their Uncertainties**

1) When you're measuring the **change** in a variable, you usually take an **initial reading** and a **final reading**.

2) This means that in order to get **one result**, you've taken **two readings** — so when you're recording your results, you'll need to take into account the **uncertainty** in **both readings**.

3) For example, when you find a **temperature change** you take two readings — the starting temperature and the final temperature. When you find the **volume** of liquid dispensed by a burette, you take an initial reading and a final reading.

4) There's a rule for dealing with uncertainties when you're combining measurements:

> If you're **adding** or **subtracting** measurements, **add** their **uncertainties.**

You can't combine percentage uncertainties like this — you have to convert them back to uncertainties first.

5) In the example at the top of the page, you're **subtracting** the initial reading from the final reading — so you need to **add together** the uncertainty in each reading.

Both burette readings have an uncertainty of ±0.05 cm³. Adding the uncertainties gives 0.05 + 0.05 = 0.1. So the uncertainty in the volume of NaOH added is **±0.1 cm³.**

This makes sense if you think about **largest** and **smallest** possible volumes of NaOH that could have been added:

The **largest** possible volume added is: 21.25 – 1.95 = **19.3 cm³**   *This is the largest possible final reading minus the smallest possible initial reading.*
The **smallest** possible volume added is: 21.15 – 2.05 = **19.1 cm³**   *This is the smallest possible final reading minus the largest possible initial reading.*

The **change in volume** is somewhere in the range of 19.1 to 19.3 cm³, or: **19.2 ±0.1 cm³**

When you're giving the **uncertainty** of a **calculated value**:

1) The **value shouldn't** be **more exact** than the **uncertainty** — e.g. if you calculated a value of 0.22 g, with an uncertainty of ±0.1 g, you should **round your value** down to give 0.2 ±0.1 g.

2) The **uncertainty shouldn't** be **more exact** than the **value** — e.g. if you calculated a value of 0.46 g, with an uncertainty of ±0.026 g, you should **round your uncertainty** up to give 0.46 ±0.03 g.

Combining Uncertainties

Worked Example

A student makes a mixture of three liquids, A, B and C. 35 cm^3 of A is measured out using a measuring cylinder with an uncertainty of ±1.0 cm^3. 65 cm^3 of B is added using a measuring cylinder with an uncertainty of ±0.5 cm^3. Finally, 25 cm^3 of C is added using a volumetric flask with a percentage uncertainty of ±0.5%.
Calculate the percentage uncertainty in the overall volume of the mixture.

1 *Convert the percentage uncertainty for the volume of liquid C back to an uncertainty.*

$$\text{uncertainty} = \frac{\text{percentage uncertainty} \times \text{reading}}{100}$$

$$= \frac{0.5 \times 25}{100}$$

$$= \pm 0.125 \text{ cm}^3$$

So you could write the volume of liquid C as **25 cm^3 ±0.125 cm^3**.

2 *Calculate the total volume of the solution.*

Total volume = 35 + 65 + 25 = **125 cm^3**

3 *Calculate the total uncertainty in the volume of the mixture.*

You're adding three measurements together, so you need to add their uncertainties.

So you could write the total volume of the mixture as **125 cm^3 ±1.625 cm^3**.

Total uncertainty = 1.0 + 0.5 + 0.125 = **1.625 cm^3**

4 *Calculate the percentage uncertainty in the volume of the mixture.*

$$\text{percentage uncertainty} = \frac{\text{uncertainty}}{\text{reading}} \times 100$$

$$= \frac{1.625}{125}$$

$$= 1.3\%$$

So you could also write the total volume of the mixture as **125 cm^3 ±1.3%**.

Practice Questions

Q1 A student burned a measured mass of a fuel in a calorimeter.
He recorded the starting temperature and the final temperature of the water in the calorimeter.
The starting temperature of the water was 20.4 ±0.2 °C. The final temperature was 45.6 ±0.2 °C.
Find the temperature change and give the uncertainty in your answer.

Q2 The pH of a weak acid was measured as 5.9 ±0.1.
Following the addition of a weak base, the pH of the solution was measured as 7.5 ±0.1.
State the change in pH and give the uncertainty in your answer.

Q3 As part of an experiment a student made up a solution of $CaCl_2$.
She measured the mass of solid $CaCl_2$ and the weighing bottle she used as 55.0 g ±0.91%.
After tipping the solid into a volumetric flask, she measured the mass of the weighing bottle as 30.0 g ±1.67%.
Find the mass of $CaCl_2$ that the student added to the flask and state total uncertainty in this measurement.

Q4 Burette A and burette B were used to add an acid and an alkali respectively to a reaction vessel.
The initial reading of burette A was 1.2 cm^3 ±0.1 cm^3 and the final reading was 25.2 cm^3 ±0.1 cm^3.
The initial reading of burette B was 2.6 cm^3 ±0.2 cm^3 and the final reading was 5.6 cm^3 ± 0.2 cm^3.
Calculate the percentage uncertainty for the overall amount of liquid added to the reaction vessel.

Chemistry and Mathematics — a lethal combination...

When adding together uncertainties make sure you are adding absolute uncertainties together and not percentage uncertainties. It's an easy mistake to make, a bit like walking into a glass door. We've all been there... oh, only me?

Using Equations and Formulae

Equations and formulae are used everywhere in chemistry to describe the relationships between quantities.
That means knowing how to use them is a pretty vital skill if you want to get through chemistry unscathed...

Equations and Formulae Show the Relationships Between Quantities

A **formula** is a just a statement that tells you the **relationship** between two or more **variables**. You'll probably already be familiar with a fair few chemistry formulae. For example:

$$\text{Number of Moles} = \frac{\text{Mass of substance (in g)}}{\text{Relative Molecular Mass, } M_r}$$

$$\text{Concentration (mol dm}^{-3}) = \frac{\text{Number of moles}}{\text{Volume of solution (dm}^3)}$$

A formula can be written out in **words**, or it may use **letters** to represent the variables. For example, you might see the first formula above written as: $n = \frac{m}{M_r}$

An **equation** is a mathematical statement which tells you that two things have an **equal value** — for example, $2x = 6$. Many formulae are written as equations.

Lots of formulae and equations crop up in chemistry, so you need to be comfortable interpreting and using them.

Bill and Phil had such an equal relationship that they frequently struggled to remember who was who.

You Need to Recognise the Symbols Used in Some Formulae

Most of the symbols that you'll come across in chemistry will be familiar, but there are a few that may be new to you:

Symbol	Meaning	Example of where you might see it being used
~	'approximately'	Stating where a peak lies on IR spectra: **There is a carboxylic acid O–H absorption peak at ~3000 cm⁻¹**
>> or <<	>> means 'is much more than', << means 'is much less than'	Used to show that the concentration of one substance is much greater than the concentration of another. For example: $[HA_{(aq)}] >> [H^+_{(aq)}]$
∝	'is directly proportional to'	For a first order reaction, rate is proportional to concentration. You can write this as: **rate ∝ [X]**
⇌	'reaction can proceed in both directions'	Used to show that a reaction is reversible, for example the Haber process: $N_2 + 3H_2 \rightleftharpoons 2NH_3$
≈	'is approximately equal to'	Used to show that the concentration of an acid at equilibrium is almost the same as it was at the start of the reaction: $[HA_{(aq)}]_{start} \approx [HA_{(aq)}]_{equilibrium}$

Make Sure Quantities are in the Correct Units

For more on units, see pages 24-29.

1) Your quantities need to be in the **correct units** before you use them in an equation — e.g. to get a concentration in mol dm⁻³ using the equation 'concentration = moles ÷ volume', you need the volume to be in dm³.

2) The overall units on each side of an equation must be the **same**. If a question specifies the answer should be in certain units, you might have to convert your quantities to appropriate units first.

3) You can **check** the units are the **same** on both sides of an equation. For example, if you're finding the rate of a reaction in **mol dm⁻³ s⁻¹** using 'rate = change in concentration ÷ time', the concentration should be in **mol dm⁻³** and the time in **s** so that both sides match.

Rate = change in concentration ÷ time
mol dm⁻³ s⁻¹ = mol dm⁻³ ÷ s

Using Equations and Formulae

Worked Example

An exothermic reaction results in an increase in the entropy of the surroundings.

This relationship is shown by the equation: $\Delta S_{surroundings} = -\dfrac{\Delta H}{T}$,

where $\Delta S_{surroundings}$ is the change in entropy of the surroundings (in J K^{-1} mol^{-1}), ΔH is the enthalpy change of the reaction (in J mol^{-1}) and T is the temperature of the surroundings (in K).

2 moles of methane are completely burnt in oxygen under standard conditions (that is a pressure of 100 kPa and a temperature of 25.0 °C). The total enthalpy change of the reaction is –1780 kJ.

Calculate the change in entropy of the surroundings for this reaction, in J K^{-1} mol^{-1}.

1 Identify and calculate the quantities to use in the equation.

To calculate the entropy change of surroundings, you need the values for ΔH and T.

As two moles are being burnt the enthalpy change per mole of methane must be half the total enthalpy change:

$\Delta H = -1780 \div 2 = \textbf{–890 kJ mol}^{-1}$

The reaction occurs at 25.0 °C, so: $T = \textbf{25.0 °C}$

2 Check the quantities are in the correct units.

To calculate entropy in J K^{-1} mol^{-1}, you need the enthalpy change in J mol^{-1} and the temperature in K.

The change in enthalpy is given in kJ mol^{-1} so you need to convert this into J mol^{-1}.

Multiply by 1000 to convert kJ into J: $\Delta H = -890 \times 1000 = \textbf{–890 000 J mol}^{-1}$

The temperature is given in °C so you need to convert this into K.

You need to add 273 to convert °C to K: $T = 273 + 25.0 = \textbf{298.0 K}$

Have a look at pages 27–29 for help on converting units.

3 Substitute the values in the correct units into the equation.

$\Delta S_{surroundings} = -\dfrac{\Delta H}{T}$ so: $\Delta S_{surroundings} = -\left(\dfrac{-890\,000}{298.0}\right) = 2986.577... = \textbf{2990 J K}^{-1}\textbf{ mol}^{-1}\textbf{ (3 s.f.)}$

Practice Questions

Q1 The number of moles in a given mass of a substance is given by the equation '$n = m \div M_r$', where n = number of moles, m = mass (in g) and M_r = relative molecular mass.
Given that the M_r of CO_2 is 44.0, calculate the number of moles in 125 g of CO_2.

Q2 The concentration of a solution can be found using the equation 'concentration = number of moles ÷ volume'. 5.0 moles of $CaCl_2$ is dissolved in 750 cm^3 of water. Calculate the concentration of the $CaCl_2$ in mol dm^{-3}.
To convert from cm^3 to dm^3, divide by 1000.

Q3 The equation $q = mc\Delta T$ is used in calorimetry experiments, where q is the heat lost or gained (in J), m is the mass of water heated (in g), c is the specific heat capacity of water (4.18 J g^{-1} K^{-1}) and ΔT is the change in temperature of the water used (in K).

16.0 g of an organic liquid, X, with $M_r = 64.0$, was completely burned in oxygen at constant pressure. The heat formed during this combustion raised the temperature of 104 g of water from 298 K to 361 K.

a) Calculate the value of q for the combustion of this sample of X. Give your answer in kJ.
b) Use the formula from Q1 to find n, the number of moles of X in 16.0 g.
c) ΔH_c, the standard enthalpy of combustion, is given by the formula $\Delta H_c = q \div n$. Find ΔH_c for the combustion of X in kJ mol^{-1}.
To convert from J to kJ, divide by 1000.

Tastiness of Cake >> Tastiness of Sprouts...

Good ol' fashioned equations, don't you just love 'em? Okay, maybe not, but they are used everywhere in chemistry so you need to know your stuff. If you struggled with the questions, have a look over the page again until it makes sense.

Rearranging Equations

With some formulae, you'll be lucky and the variable you're trying to find will already be on one side of the formula on its own. Often though, you'll have to do some rearranging first to get the variable that you want on its own...

Rearranging an Equation Shows the Same Relationship in a Different Way

You know that: **number of moles = mass ÷ M_r**

You can also say: **mass = number of moles × M_r**

and: **M_r = mass ÷ number of moles**

These equations all show the **same relationship** — they've just been **rearranged**.

When you're doing calculations in chemistry, you'll quite often have to rearrange formulae like these before you use them. So it's really important to make sure that you're comfortable with how to do it.

There's One Golden Rule for Rearranging Equations

Whatever you do to **one side** of the equation, you need to do to the **other side** of the equation.

This includes things like adding, subtracting, multiplying, dividing, as well as trickier things like squaring, taking a square root or a logarithm.

For example, to rearrange $c = \dfrac{n}{v}$ (concentration = number of moles ÷ volume) to find v:

1) **Multiply** both sides by v: $c \times v = \dfrac{n}{v} \times v$ — The 'v's cancel out.

$cv = n$

2) **Divide** both sides by c: $\dfrac{cv}{c} = \dfrac{n}{c}$

$v = \dfrac{n}{c}$

So $v = \dfrac{n}{c}$

If you need to rearrange an equation, you should normally do this **before** you substitute in your values. It can be a bit trickier to rearrange an equation once you've substituted all the numbers into it.

Worked Example 1

The ideal gas equation $pV = nRT$, lets you approximately find the number of moles in a certain volume of gas, where p is the pressure in Pa, V is the volume in m³, n is the number of moles, R is the gas constant (8.31 J K⁻¹ mol⁻¹) and T is the temperature in K.

A gas occupies a volume of 4.80 m³ at a temperature of 298 K and a pressure of 1250 Pa.
Calculate the number of moles of gas. The gas constant is 8.31 J K⁻¹ mol⁻¹.

1 *Identify the quantity that you need to find*

You want to find the number of moles, which is n.

2 *Rearrange the equation to get n on its own.*

$pV = nRT$ → $\dfrac{pV}{R} = nT$ → $\dfrac{pV}{RT} = n$

Divide both sides by R. Divide both sides by T.

Although Hilda would never admit it, she wanted to rearrange her marriage.

Rearranging Equations

3 *Substitute in your values to find n.*

$$n = \frac{1250 \times 4.80}{8.31 \times 298}$$

$$n = 2.422....$$

$n = 2.42$ moles (to 3 s.f.)

Make sure you check the units before substituting the values into the equation.

Worked Example 2

Free energy change, ΔG, is used to predict whether or not a reaction is feasible.
For any given reaction $\Delta G = \Delta H - T\Delta S$, where ΔG = free energy change, ΔH = enthalpy change of the system, T = temperature of the surroundings and ΔS = entropy change of the system.
ΔS can be calculated using the equation $\Delta S = S_{products} - S_{reactants}$,
where $S_{products}$ = sum of the entropies of the products and $S_{reactants}$ = sum of the entropies of the reactants.

Carbon monoxide and water vapour can form carbon dioxide and hydrogen gas in a reversible reaction:

$$CO_{(g)} + H_2O_{(g)} \rightleftharpoons CO_{2(g)} + H_{2(g)}$$

Calculate $S_{products}$, given that $\Delta G = -28\,648$ J mol^{-1}, $\Delta H = -41.2$ kJ mol^{-1}, $T = 298$ K and $S_{reactants} = 386.5$ J mol^{-1} K^{-1}.

---

1 *Identify the quantity that you need to find.*

You want to find $S_{products}$, the sum of the entropies of the products.

2 *Rearrange $\Delta S = S_{products} - S_{reactants}$ to get $S_{products}$ on its own.*

$$\Delta S = S_{products} - S_{reactants} \qquad\longrightarrow\qquad \Delta S + S_{reactants} = S_{products}$$

Add $S_{reactants}$ to both sides.

You know $S_{reactants}$ but you need to find the value of ΔS before you can use this formula.

3 *Rearrange $\Delta G = \Delta H - T\Delta S$ to get ΔS on its own.*

To find $S_{products}$, you first need to find ΔS. So next you need to rearrange the ΔG formula to get ΔS on its own:

$$\Delta G = \Delta H - T\Delta S \longrightarrow \Delta G + T\Delta S = \Delta H \longrightarrow T\Delta S = \Delta H - \Delta G \longrightarrow \Delta S = \frac{\Delta H - \Delta G}{T}$$

Add $T\Delta S$ to both sides.

Subtract ΔG from both sides.

Divide both sides by T.

You know the values of ΔH, ΔG and T, so you can use this equation to find ΔS.

4 *Check the quantities are in the correct units.*

You want to calculate ΔS in J K^{-1} mol^{-1}. ΔH is in kJ mol^{-1}, so convert it to J mol^{-1} by multiplying by 1000.

See pages 27-29 for more on converting units.

$$\Delta H = -41.2 \text{ kJ mol}^{-1} = (-41.2 \times 1000) \text{ J mol}^{-1}$$

$$= -41\,200 \text{ J mol}^{-1}$$

5 *Substitute in your values to find ΔS.*

$$\Delta S = \frac{\Delta H - \Delta G}{T} = \frac{-41\,200 - (-28\,648)}{298} = \frac{-41\,200 + 28\,648}{298} = \frac{-12\,552}{298} = -42.12... \text{ J K}^{-1} \text{ mol}^{-1}$$

6 *Substitute in your value for ΔS in to $S_{products} = \Delta S + S_{reactants}$*

$$S_{products} = \Delta S + S_{reactants}$$

$$= -42.12... + 386.5$$

$$= 344.397... = 344 \text{ J K}^{-1} \text{ mol}^{-1} \text{ (to 3 s.f.)}$$

Rearranging Equations

Some Equations are a Bit *Tricky* to Rearrange

Some equations you'll meet will be more complicated and will include fractions, powers and logs.

These might be a bit more difficult to solve and will include some extra steps in order to rearrange so you get what you want on its own on one side of the equation.

> For example, if $[H_2]^2 = 15$, then to find $[H_2]$, take the square root of both sides: $[H_2] = \sqrt{15}$.
> You can find this using your calculator: $\boxed{\sqrt{}}\ \boxed{1}\ \boxed{5}\ \boxed{=}$ $\quad \sqrt{15}$
> $\qquad\qquad\qquad\qquad\qquad\qquad\qquad\qquad\qquad\qquad 3.872983346$

This is a 'second function' on some calculators, so you might have to press shift or second function first.

Worked Example 3

Nitrogen dioxide, NO_2, decomposes to form nitric oxide, NO, and oxygen, O_2 according to this equation:

$$2NO_{2(g)} \rightarrow NO_{(g)} + O_{2(g)}$$

The rate of this reaction is given by the equation: Rate $= k[NO_2]^2$,
where k is the rate constant and $[NO_2]$ is the concentration of NO_2.

A student conducted an experiment with an unknown concentration of nitrogen dioxide.
At 500 K the rate was found to be 2.50×10^{-3} mol dm^{-3} s^{-1} and k was calculated at 1.20×10^{-2} dm^3 mol^{-1} s^{-1}.
Calculate the concentration of NO_2 for this reaction.

1 *Identify the quantity that you need to find.*
You want to find the concentration of NO_2, which is $[NO_2]$.

2 *Rearrange the equation to get $[NO_2]^2$ on its own.*
Before you can get rid of the power, you need to get $[NO_2]^2$ on its own.

$$\text{Rate} = k[NO_2]^2 \quad \longrightarrow \quad \frac{\text{Rate}}{k} = [NO_2]^2$$

Divide both sides by k.

3 *Take the inverse of the power for both sides of the equation.*
Now, to get $[NO_2]$ on its own, you need to take the square root of both sides of the equation.

$$\frac{\text{Rate}}{k} = [NO_2]^2 \quad \longrightarrow \quad \sqrt{\frac{\text{Rate}}{k}} = \sqrt{[NO_2]^2} \quad \longrightarrow \quad \sqrt{\frac{\text{Rate}}{k}} = [NO_2]$$

Take the square root of both sides.

The square root and the power cancel each other out.

4 *Substitute your values in to find $[NO_2]$.*

$$[NO_2] = \sqrt{\left(\frac{2.50 \times 10^{-3}}{1.20 \times 10^{-2}}\right)} = \sqrt{0.208333\ldots} = 0.456435\ldots = \textbf{0.456 mol dm}^{-3}\ \textbf{(3 s.f.)}$$

Rearranging Equations

Worked Example 4

The free energy of a reaction and its equilibrium constant are related via this formula: $\Delta G = -RT \ln K$
ΔG is the change in free energy for the reaction (in J mol⁻¹), R is the gas constant (8.31 J K⁻¹ mol⁻¹),
T is the temperature (in K) and K is the equilibrium constant.

The Haber Process is used to form ammonia via the reaction $N_2 + 3H_2 \rightleftharpoons 2NH_3$.
For this reaction at 298 K, $\Delta G = -16\,480$ J mol⁻¹. Calculate the value of K. The units of K are mol⁻² dm⁶.

1 **Identify the quantity that you need to find.**

You want to find the equilibrium constant, which is K.

2 **Rearrange the equation to get ln K on its own.**

Before you can get rid of the natural logarithm, you need to get $\ln K$ on its own.

$$\Delta G = -RT \ln K \qquad \longrightarrow \qquad \frac{\Delta G}{-RT} = \ln K$$

Divide both
sides by $-RT$.

*For more on
natural logarithms,
see pages 22-23.*

3 **Take the inverse of the natural logarithm.**

Now, to get K on its own, you need to find the inverse of $\ln K$.
To do this, you need to take the exponential function (e^x, see page 22) of both sides of the equation.

$$\ln K = \frac{\Delta G}{-RT} \longrightarrow e^{\ln K} = e^{\frac{\Delta G}{-RT}} \longrightarrow K = e^{\frac{\Delta G}{-RT}}$$

Take the exponential $e \ln K = K$, so...
function of both sides

4 **Substitute your values in to find K.**

$$K = e^{\frac{\Delta G}{-RT}} = e^{\frac{-16\,480}{-8.31 \times 298}}$$

$$K = e^{6.6549\ldots} = 776.561\ldots = \mathbf{780 \text{ mol}^{-2} \text{ dm}^6 \text{ (2 s.f.)}}$$

Practice Questions

Q1 The formula 'concentration = $\dfrac{\text{number of moles}}{\text{volume}}$' is used to calculate the concentration of a solution.

A student want to make a solution of NaOH with a concentration of 7.5×10^{-3} mol dm⁻³
using 2.5×10^{-3} moles of NaOH.
Calculate the volume of water needed to make a solution with the correct concentration.

Q2 The behaviour of an ideal gas is represented by the equation $pV = nRT$, where p is the pressure (in Pa),
V is the volume (in m³), n is the number of moles of the gas, R is the gas constant (8.31 J K⁻¹ mol⁻¹)
and T is the temperature (in K).

5.6 moles of nitrogen gas are kept at a temperature of 350 K and at a pressure of 12 000 Pa.
Calculate the volume of the gas.

Q3 Hydrogen gas and iodine gas are mixed together in a closed flask, forming hydrogen iodide.
The equilibrium constant expression for the reaction is shown below.

$$K_c = \frac{[HI]^2}{[H_2][I_2]}$$

[X] means concentration of X in mol dm⁻³.

If, at equilibrium, $[H_2] = 0.228$ mol dm⁻³, $[I_2] = 0.228$ mol dm⁻³ and $K_c = 45.9$, calculate [HI].

Rearrange this well known phrase — Learn page everything on this...

*So this is a bit more difficult than the previous page. Do not fear, my chemically advanced maths adventurer. If you're
struggling with rearranging equations that include logs, have a recap of the rules of logs on pages 20-23 and come back
here and go through the worked examples. I'm 99.9% sure you won't regret it. And if you do, have some chocolate.*

Plotting Graphs

Often when you've done an experiment, you'll need to draw a graph. Not only are they a nifty way of displaying any experimental results, they're pretty much guaranteed to come up in your exams. So make sure you know the basics.

Graphs Show a **Relationship** Between **Variables**

When you carry out experiments in chemistry, you'll often be measuring what happens to one **variable** when another variable is changed.

For example, you might measure the volume of carbon dioxide gas produced over the course of a reaction between calcium carbonate and hydrochloric acid. **Volume** and **time** are the variables in this case.

Time / s	0	30	60	90	120	150
Volume of CO_2 produced / cm³	0.00	7.00	15.75	17.75	19.00	19.50

It can be hard to tell what's going on just from a results table — so you can plot your results on a **graph** too:

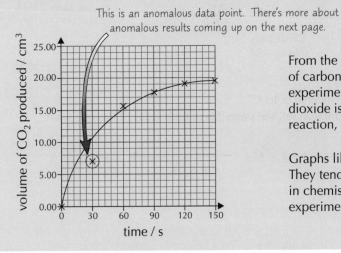

This is an anomalous data point. There's more about anomalous results coming up on the next page.

From the graph, its **really easy** to see that the volume of carbon dioxide **increases** over the course of the experiment. You can also easily see that carbon dioxide is produced more quickly at the start of the reaction, and slows down as the reaction continues.

Graphs like this are called **scatter graphs**. They tend to be the most useful graphs in chemistry when it comes to plotting experimental results.

Make Sure you can **Plot** a **Scatter Graph**

Here are some simple steps to follow when it comes to plotting a scatter graph...

1) Identify which variable is the **independent variable**, and which is the **dependent variable**.

> The **independent variable** is the thing you **change**.
> The **dependent variable** is the thing you **measure**.

A variable is any quantity that can change in an experiment.

In the example above, time is the independent variable, and the volume of carbon dioxide produced is the dependent variable.

You're not exactly changing time yourself here, but you are measuring the effect of time changing on the volume of CO_2 produced — so time is still the independent variable.

Generally speaking, the **independent variable** will go **along the bottom** of your graph (the *x*-axis) and the **dependent variable** will go **up the side** of your graph (the *y*-axis).

2) Choose a **sensible scale** for your graph by looking at the **range** of your data.

> The scale you should use will depend on how much **room** you've got. You want your graph to be **easy to read**, so nice and **big**, but you also need your **scale** to be **sensible** so that you can read it easily, and plot your points without too much difficulty.

In the example above, on the *y*-axis, 1 division = 1.0 cm³, which is a nice, easy scale to work with.

On the *x*-axis, 5 divisions = 30 seconds, so 1 division = 30 ÷ 5 = 6 seconds. This is a bit trickier, but it's the kind of scale you may have to use if space is limited or a variable has an awkward range.

Plotting Graphs

3) **Draw** and **label** your axes, then **plot your data** with a sharp pencil.

Don't forget to include the **units** on your axes.

You should separate the units from the axis name using a **slash** (/) or **brackets**.

Mark each data point with a cross.

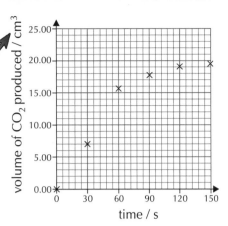

Plotting graphs was all very well and good, but Mittens preferred plotting world domination.

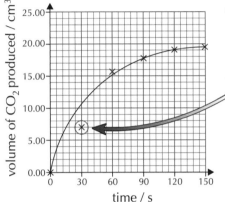

4) Draw a **line of best fit** to show the trend in your data.

You should aim to have the **same number** of points below the line as above it, with the line passing through **as many points as possible**.

Keep an eye out for any points that **don't fit** the general trend of your data, like this one. These are called **anomalous results**, and they are generally caused by mistakes in the experiment. You should **ignore** anomalous results when you're drawing the line of best fit.

If your line of best fit is curved, make sure that the curve is **smooth**. (If it helps, try turning the paper upside-down to draw it.)

Strictly speaking, in maths, 'line' means a straight line. You might have been taught in GCSE maths that lines of best fit should always be straight — but scientists tend to use 'line of best fit' for curves too. Just don't tell your maths teacher...

Worked Example

The data in the table on the right shows how the absorbance of a solution changes as the concentration of an aqueous metal ion is varied.

Draw a graph to show how the absorbance varies with the concentration of the aqueous metal ion, and draw a line of best fit.

Concentration of metal ion / mol dm⁻³	0.00	0.01	0.02	0.03	0.04	0.05
Absorbance	0.00	0.23	0.47	0.74	1.02	1.25

Absorbance doesn't have any units.

1 *Figure out which variable goes on which axis.*

You're looking at how absorbance changes as you vary concentration, so the concentration of the metal ion is the independent variable and absorbance is the dependent variable. This means:

Concentration should go on the **x-axis** and absorbance should go on the **y-axis**.

2 *Pick sensible scales.*

You need the data to be **spread out** enough to see what's going on and the scale to be **easy to use** for your data.

- For the x-axis, the concentration measurements go up in steps of 0.01 mol dm⁻³. A scale of one square = 0.002 mol dm⁻³ will put every data point on a major grid line.
- This will spread the x-axis data across at least five large squares. ⟸ In this case, 1 large square = 5 small squares.
- For the y-axis, the absorbance measurements don't go up in even steps. But they are all measured to two decimal places, so a scale of one square = 0.02 will mean that every point will either be on a grid line or exactly halfway between two grid lines. This should make the data easy to plot.
- This scale will spread the y-axis across at least thirteen large squares, which also seems reasonable.

So the scales will be:

1 square = 0.002 mol dm⁻³ for the **concentration** (x) axis.
1 square = 0.02 units of absorbance for the **absorbance** (y) axis.

Scales should always go up in regular intervals.

SECTION 5 — GRAPH SKILLS

Plotting Graphs

③ Draw the graph.

First draw the graph axes using the scales you've chosen.
Make sure you clearly label the axes with the correct variables and any units.

Then plot the data points using a sharp pencil.

④ Draw a line of best fit.

Draw a line of best fit to show the trend in your data.

These scales work well — they give you a big graph and most of the points are on grid lines rather than between them. The points all fall on major (thick) grid lines for the x-axis, which makes the graph much easier to draw.

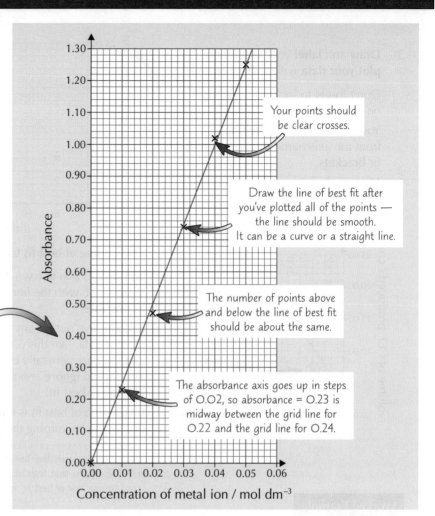

Your points should be clear crosses.

Draw the line of best fit after you've plotted all of the points — the line should be smooth. It can be a curve or a straight line.

The number of points above and below the line of best fit should be about the same.

The absorbance axis goes up in steps of 0.02, so absorbance = 0.23 is midway between the grid line for 0.22 and the grid line for 0.24.

You might also meet line graphs — they look a bit like scatter graphs, but all the points are joined up one-by-one instead of the graph having a line of best fit. They're usually used to show the trends on a graph where the independent variable is discrete (i.e. it can only take certain specific values). You might be asked to interpret a line graph, e.g. a graph showing a trend in a physical property of some elements across the periodic table, but it's very unlikely you'll have to draw one.

Practice Questions

Q1 A student is carrying out an experiment to monitor the change in pH of a solution over time.
In order to analyse her data, she wishes to plot the data on a graph.

a) What should she plot on the x-axis of her graph?

b) What should she plot on the y-axis of her graph?

Q2 The data in the table below shows how concentration of a product, D, changed over the course of a reaction.

Time / s	0	20	40	60	80	100	120
Concentration of product D / mol dm⁻³	0.00	0.80	1.35	1.70	1.85	1.90	1.93

Plot a graph using this data. Include a line of best fit on your graph.

Warning — this section contains graphic content...

It's easy to get a bit over-confident when you're drawing graphs, so take care. If you make a mistake, anything you work out from your graph (e.g. the gradient — see page 52) will also be incorrect. So, take a few deep breaths, put your concentration hat on, and take the time now to really get to grips with plotting graphs. You'll thank me in the long run.

Interpreting Graphs

It's all well and good being able to take a load of data and turn it into a pretty graph. But now it's time to learn how to interpret graphs. I promise you, hidden in those little crosses, lines and axes there's a whole load of chemistry...

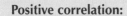

A **Correlation** Describes the **Relationship** Between Two **Variables**

There are three different kinds of **correlation** you need to be able to recognise:

Positive correlation:

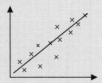

As one variable increases the other increases. Similarly, if one variable decreases, the other variable decreases.

Negative correlation:

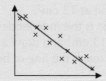

As one variable increases, the other decreases.

No correlation:

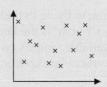

There is no relationship between the variables — there is no pattern in the data.

If you do find a **correlation**, you need to decide whether the effect you're seeing is **caused** by changing the independent variable (this is known as a **causal relationship**). There may be **another variable** that is changing **at the same time** as the independent variable and is causing the change in the dependent variable.

You Need to Be Able to **Read Data** From Graphs

Reading data from graphs is pretty straightforward if you know how to plot them. You just need to make sure you don't get the quantities on the *x*-axis and the *y*-axis mixed up, and that you **read the scales** properly.

The graph below shows how the mass of a beaker (and the reaction mixture in it) varies with time. Here's how you'd find the mass of the beaker after 40 seconds:

1) The time on the *x*-axis is in seconds, so find **40** on the *x*-axis and draw a line **up** to the **line of best fit**.

2) Then draw a line **across** from the line of best fit to the *y*-axis to find the mass. This line meets the *y*-axis one square below 230 g.

3) On this axis, 5 squares = 10 grams, so **one square** = 10 ÷ 5 = **2 grams**. The mass measurement for the red data point is 230 – 2 = **228 g**.

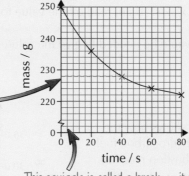

This squiggle is called a break — it shows that some values have been missed out on this axis. You can use a break to miss out a range of values on an axis that are lower than the lowest data value.

So the red data point shows that, after **40 seconds**, the reaction beaker has a mass of **228 g**.

The point in the example above happened to be a plotted data point on the graph, but you can also read off the value of points on the line of best fit that lie **between** data points. This is known as **interpolation**.

You don't just have to stick to reading off data points from within the range of known values either. You can **extend** the line of best fit outside of the range covered by your data. This is known as **extrapolation**. This can be useful to predict the value of a variable without having to redo your experiment to include the value you're interested in.

Extrapolation generally isn't quite as accurate as interpolation, because it assumes that the trend shown by your line of best fit remains correct beyond the range of the data that you've measured.

SECTION 5 — GRAPH SKILLS

Interpreting Graphs

Worked Example 1

The graph on the right is a pH curve from a titration between a strong acid and a strong base.

a) Predict what the pH of the solution will be when 13 cm³ of acid have been added?

1 Find the known variable on the correct axis.

You're trying to find the pH of the solution at 13 cm³, so 13 cm³ is the known variable. Volume is the independent variable, and it's on the *x*-axis. So, find 13 cm³ and draw a vertical line up from this point until you reach the line of best fit.

2 Read across from the line of best fit to find the unknown.

Once you've reached the line of best fit, you need to draw a line straight across to the *y*-axis. Then read off the value for *y* at this point.

> When 13 cm³ of acid has been added the pH will be **4.8**.

b) Estimate the volume of acid that would be needed to give the solution a pH of 11.8.

3 Find the known variable on the correct axis.

This time, you're trying to find the volume from the pH. pH is on the *y*-axis, so find pH = 11.8 and draw a horizontal line across from this point, until you reach the line of best fit.

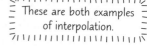

4 Read down from the line of best fit to find the unknown.

Once you've reached the line of best fit, you need to draw a line straight down until you reach the *x*-axis. Then, read off the value for *x* at this point.

> **8.0 cm³** of acid would be needed to give the solution a pH of 11.8.

These are both examples of interpolation.

Worked Example 2

The graph on the right shows how the mass of a sample of a hydrocarbon fuel changes during a combustion reaction.
Predict what mass of the hydrocarbon fuel will be left after 8 minutes.

1 Extrapolate the line of best fit.

You'll need to **extend** your line of best fit so it passes beyond the range of the your own data, to at least 8 minutes (the point that you're interested in).

When extrapolating your line of best fit, try and match it as closely as possible to the trend shown by the line of best fit that was drawn within your data. If it's a straight line, remember to use a ruler.

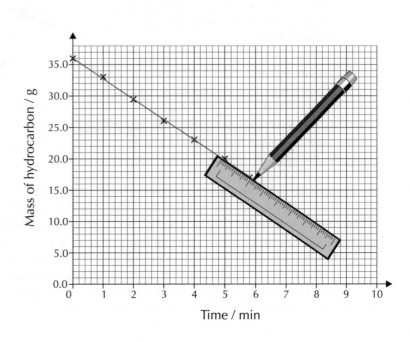

Interpreting Graphs

2 ***Find the known variable on the correct axis.***

As in the example on the opposite page, the next step is to find the known variable on the relevant axis. In this case, you're looking for the mass at **8 minutes**, so start by finding 8 minutes on the *x*-axis. Then, draw a line straight up from this point, until you find the line of best fit.

3 ***Read across from the line of best fit to find the unknown.***

Now it's plain sailing. Once you've reached the line of best fit, draw a horizontal line, until you reach the *y*-axis. Then, read off the value for *y* at this point.

10.0 g of the hydrocarbon fuel will be left after 8 minutes.

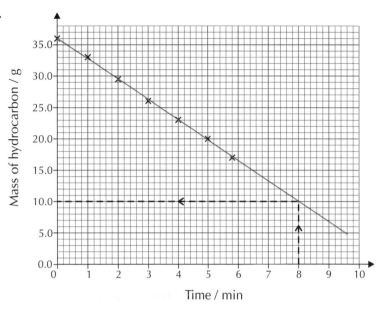

Extrapolation only works for graphs where there's a clear trend with strong correlation (this is where most of the data points sit close to, or on, the line of best fit).

Tommy's new Spring/Summer clothing range was a clothing line of loose fit.

Practice Questions

Q1 The graph on the right shows the change in temperature over time when a measured mass of zinc powder was added to a known concentration of aqueous copper(II) sulfate.

    a) Describe what happens to the temperature over the course of the experiment.

    b) What temperature was the reaction mixture at 65 s?

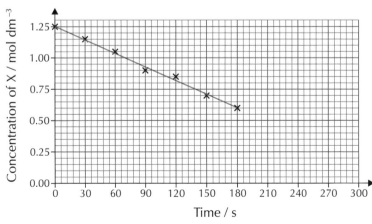

Q2 The graph on the left shows how the concentration of a reactant, X, varies over the course of an experiment.

    a) State whether the graph shows positive correlation, negative correlation or no correlation.

    b) Predict what the concentration of reactant X will be after 276 seconds.

My revision concentration-time graph shows negative correlation...

Take a good look at these pages. A good, long, hard look... That correlation stuff will be pretty handy, but I'll bet my bottom dollar that you'll have some sort of graph to interpret in your exams. It's not too hard, just make sure you're armed with a ruler — this will make it so much easier to read up or along from a point on an axis to the line of best fit.

Linear Graphs

So you've plotted your data and drawn a line of best fit... The next step is to find the gradient and the intercept.

The **Gradient** of a **Linear Graph** is **Constant**

The **gradient** of a graph is a measure of **how steep** the line is — the steeper the line, the larger the gradient.

The gradient of a graph tells you the **rate of change** of the quantity on the **y-axis** with respect to the quantity on the **x-axis**. This tells you how much a change in the x-axis **variable** affects the y-axis variable.

Often, the gradient of a graph is a **useful quantity**. E.g. the gradient of the concentration-time graph of a reaction is equal to the rate of the reaction.

When a graph is a **straight line**, its gradient is **constant**. This means you can find its gradient using any pair of points on the graph (see below).

[X] means 'the concentration of substance X'.

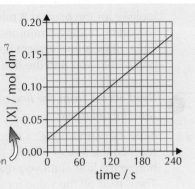

You Can Write an **Equation** for a **Straight Line**

A **linear graph** has the **equation**: $y = mx + c$ Where **m** is the **gradient** and **c** is the **y-intercept** — the value of y when x = 0.

The **gradient**, *m*, is the change in the variable on the y-axis divided by the change in the variable on the x-axis:

$$m = \frac{\text{change in } y}{\text{change in } x}$$

Sometimes in chemistry, you only need the size of the gradient and can ignore the sign — but in other cases the sign does matter.

A linear graph that slopes upwards from left to right has a positive gradient. If the graph slopes downwards from left to right, the gradient is negative.

Make Sure You Can **Find m** and **c** From a **Graph**

Here's how to find the gradient of a **linear** graph, using the graph shown below as an example:

1) Pick a **part of the line** to work with. Ideally, it should be a reasonably big section of the line and start and end at points where grid lines cross — that way their x-axis and y-axis values will be easy to read off, so you'll be able to calculate the gradient as **accurately** as possible.

Here, the section from 60 s to 180 s looks good.

2) Draw a **right-angled triangle**, with your section of the line as the **hypotenuse** (the longest side).

3) Work out how much the **y variable changes** over the section you're looking at.

This is the height of your triangle.

   change in y = 0.14 − 0.06 = **0.08 mol dm⁻³**

4) Work out how much the **x variable changes** over the same section.

This is the base of your triangle.

   change in x = 180 − 60 = **120 s**

Always take away the x and y values for the left-hand side of the triangle from those for the right-hand side. This means the change in x will always be positive, but the change in y could be positive or negative.

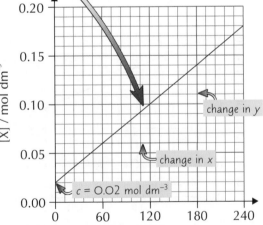

5) Find $\frac{\text{change in } y}{\text{change in } x}$. This is the **gradient**, *m*.

   $m = \frac{\text{change in } y}{\text{change in } x} = 0.08 \div 120 = 7 \times 10^{-4} \text{ mol dm}^{-3} \text{ s}^{-1}$ **(to 1 s.f.)**

6) The **y-intercept**, *c*, is the value on the y-axis where the line crosses it.

   c = **0.02 mol dm⁻³**

There's more about how you work out the units for calculations like these on page 24.

Linear Graphs

Worked Example

The graph on the right shows the relationship between free energy change (ΔG) and temperature (T) for a certain reaction. The y-intercept of the graph is equal to ΔH, the enthalpy change of the reaction, and the gradient is equal to $-\Delta S$, where ΔS is the entropy change of the reaction.

For the reaction represented by this graph, find:

a)   **the entropy change of the reaction in kJ K^{-1} mol^{-1},**

b)   **the enthalpy change of the reaction in kJ mol^{-1}.**

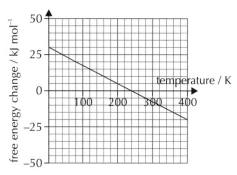

1 *Pick a part of the line to use to calculate the gradient.*

The part of the graph between 40 K and 360 K looks good — the grid lines cross the graph at 40 K and 360 K so the values will be nice and easy to read off.

Try to pick values that are quite far apart, so you're calculating the gradient using a large amount of the graph.

2 *Draw a triangle to find the change in y and the change in x.*

Subtract the x and y values on the left-hand side of the triangle from those on the right.

change in y = –15 – 25 = –40 kJ mol^{-1} change in x = 360 – 40 = 320 K

The change in y is negative because y decreases as x increases.

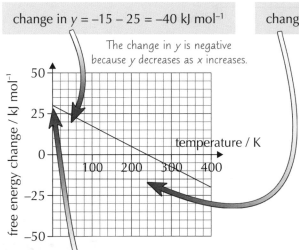

3 *Calculate the gradient.*

The gradient, m, is equal to $-\Delta S$, so the answer to part a) is $-m$.

$$m = \frac{\text{change in } y}{\text{change in } x} = -40 \div 320$$
$$= -0.125 \text{ kJ } K^{-1} \text{ mol}^{-1}$$

$m = -\Delta S$,   so $\Delta S = -m = -(-0.125)$ kJ K^{-1} mol^{-1}

$$\Delta S = 0.125 \text{ kJ } K^{-1} \text{ mol}^{-1}$$

4 *Find the y-intercept of the graph.*
This is the value of ΔH. $\Delta H = 30$ kJ mol^{-1}

Practice Question

Q1   The graph shows the change in the concentration of a chemical, Z, during the first 90 s of a reaction.

a)   Is Z a product or a reactant in this reaction? Explain your answer.

b)   Use the graph to find the rate of the reaction in mol dm^{-3} s^{-1} during this time period.

The rate of a reaction is equal to the gradient of a concentration-time graph of one of its products or reactants.

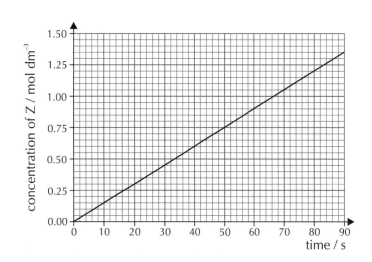

Good gradients can lead to good grades...

In the example above, it matters if the gradient is positive or negative — it tells you if the entropy increases or decreases. On the other hand, reaction rates are always given as positive values, so for rates you can ignore the sign of the gradient.

SECTION 5 — GRAPH SKILLS

Curved Graphs and Tangents

*Finding the gradient of a curved graph is a bit trickier than finding the **gradient** of a linear graph, but you still need to be able to do it. Make sure you're happy with pages 52-53 before you start this lot — it'll make it easier.*

The **Gradient** of a **Curved Graph** Is Always **Changing**

Gradients tell you the effect of a change in the x-axis variable on the y-axis variable.

The gradient of a curved graph **changes** — it is not a constant. This means that a fixed change in the x-axis variable **doesn't** cause a fixed change in the y-axis variable — so the rate of change varies along the curve.

This concentration-time graph shows how [A] (the concentration of substance A) changes during a reaction:

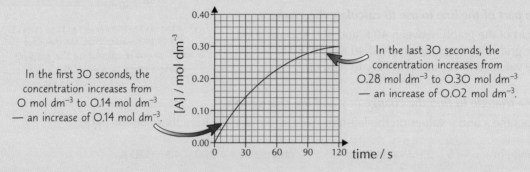

In the first 30 seconds, the concentration increases from 0 mol dm^{-3} to 0.14 mol dm^{-3} — an increase of 0.14 mol dm^{-3}.

In the last 30 seconds, the concentration increases from 0.28 mol dm^{-3} to 0.30 mol dm^{-3} — an increase of 0.02 mol dm^{-3}.

The concentration initially increases quickly, but as time goes on it increases more gradually.

The gradient of a concentration-time graph is the rate of the reaction, so the graph shows the rate is initially high, but it falls over time.

You can find the **gradient** at any **point** on a non-linear graph like this by drawing a **tangent** to the curve.

Draw a **Tangent** to a Curve to Find the **Rate of Change** at a Point

1) The gradient of a curved graph **changes** as you move along the curve. You can find the gradient at a given point by drawing a **tangent** to the curve at that point.

2) A tangent is a **straight line** that **just touches** the curve at the point you're interested in. It has the **same gradient** as the curve at that point. This means that you can find the gradient of the curve at a point by finding the gradient of its tangent.

I don't like this changing gradiiieeent!

To draw a tangent to a curve on a graph, you just need to follow these steps:

1) Find the point on the graph where you want to know the gradient.

2) Put a ruler on the graph so that it's **just touching** that point.

3) Angle the ruler so the space between the ruler and the curve is **the same** on **either side** of the point.

4) Draw a line along the ruler using a **sharp pencil**.

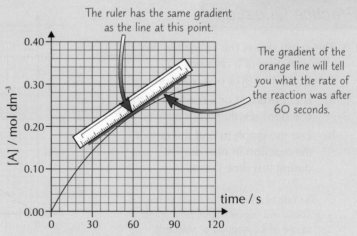

The ruler has the same gradient as the line at this point.

The gradient of the orange line will tell you what the rate of the reaction was after 60 seconds.

Then you can find the gradient of the tangent as you would for any straight line (see pages 52-53).

Just find the change in x and the change in y, then find the gradient (m) using $m = \dfrac{\text{change in } y}{\text{change in } x}$.

Curved Graphs and Tangents

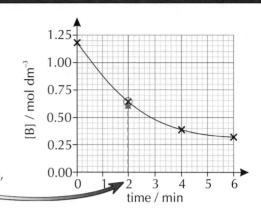

Worked Example

The graph on the right shows the change in the concentration of reactant B over the first 6 minutes of an experiment.

What was the rate of the reaction after 2 minutes?
(Give your answer in mol dm^{-3} min^{-1}.)

1 *Find the point on the curve that you need to look at.*

The question asks about the rate of the reaction after 2 minutes, so find 2 on the *x*-axis and go up to the curve from there.

2 *Place a ruler at that point so that it's just touching the curve.*

Position the ruler so you can see the whole curve.

3 *Adjust the ruler until the space between the ruler and the curve is equal on both sides of the point.*

4 *Draw a line along the ruler to make the tangent.*

Extend the line right across the graph — it'll help to make your gradient calculation easier as you'll have more points to choose from.

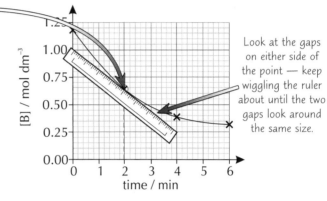

Look at the gaps on either side of the point — keep wiggling the ruler about until the two gaps look around the same size.

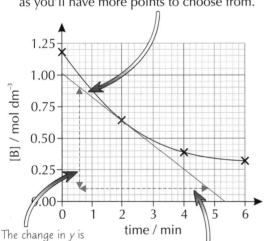

The change in *y* is
0.10 – 0.90
= **–0.80 mol dm^{-3}**.

The change in *x* is
4.8 – 0.6 = **4.2 minutes**.

5 *Calculate the gradient of the tangent to find the rate.*

You can work out the gradient using this formula:

gradient = change in *y* ÷ change in *x*

gradient = –0.80 mol dm^{-3} ÷ 4.2 min
= –0.1904... mol dm^{-3} min^{-1}
So rate = **0.19 mol dm^{-3} min^{-1} (to 2 s.f.)**

The gradient is negative, but rate of reaction is always given as a positive value, so you can ignore the minus sign for the final answer here.

Practice Question

Q1 The graph on the right shows the change in concentration of a product, C, for the first 6 minutes of a certain reaction. The reaction was carried out twice, once at a temperature of 280 K and once at a temperature of 350 K.

Calculate the rate of the reaction after 1 minute for each of the two temperatures.

Remember, the rate of reaction at a particular point is equal to the gradient of the graph at that point.

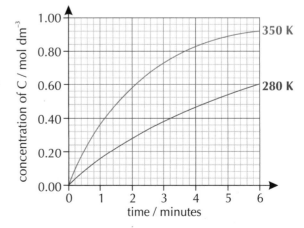

My science teacher was always going off on a tangent...

Drawing a tangent may look tricky, but all it takes is a ruler and a bit of practice. Then you can find the gradient using the same method as for a linear graph. Just remember that the tangent only gives you the gradient for one point on the curve.

Drawing Molecules in 3D

Sometimes, when you're drawing a molecule, you want to be able to show how its atoms are actually arranged in 3D. That's not the easiest thing to do on a 2D sheet of paper. But fear not, there is a way — read on...

You Can **Draw Molecules** in **2D** or in **3D**

In chemistry, you often use **displayed formulas** to represent a molecule.

A displayed formula just shows all of the **atoms** in a molecule, and the **bonds** that hold them together. Each bond is represented by a straight line.

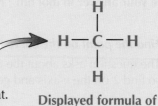

Displayed formula of
methane (CH_4)

A displayed formula is a **2D representation** of a molecule. It gives you information about what atoms are in the molecule and what's bonded to what. But it **doesn't** tell you anything about the **3D structure** of the molecule.

For example you might think from looking at the displayed formula of methane that it was flat — but the shape of a molecule of methane is actually something like this:

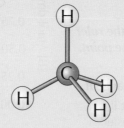

A molecule's **3D shape** is important because it affects the molecule's **physical properties** and how it **reacts**. So it's useful to have a way of representing the 3D shape of a molecule on paper.

Different Types of **Line** Represent Bonds Pointing in Different **Directions**

There are a few rules you need to know for drawing 3D representations of molecules.

1) A wedge shape shows a bond that's sticking out of the page (pointing towards you).

2) A dotted line shows a bond that's going into the page (pointing away from you).

3) An ordinary line shows a bond that's in the same plane as the page (not pointing towards you or away from you).

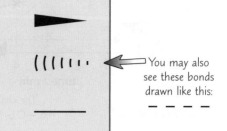
You may also
see these bonds
drawn like this:

So if you wanted to show the shape of the methane molecule above, you would draw it like this:

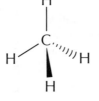

The name's Eagle...
Bond Eagle.

Bond Angles

1) When you draw a diagram to show the 3D shape of a molecule, you should include the **bond angles**.

2) A bond angle is just the angle, in degrees, between two of the bonds in a molecule. You label it like this:

3) If several of the bond angles in a molecule are the same, you can just label one — anyone looking at your diagram will assume that any unmarked angles are the same. For example, the angle between each pair of CH bonds in a methane molecule is 109.5°, so you only need to label one bond angle.

Drawing Molecules in 3D

You Need to Know How to *Draw the Shapes* of Different *Molecules*

1) The shape of a molecule is determined by how many **electron pairs** it has around its **central atom**.

2) Electron pairs can either be **bonding** (i.e. they form a bond between two atoms) or **non-bonding**. Non-bonding electrons are often called **lone pairs**. They are shown as a pair of either **crosses** or **dots**, like this: ×× or ••. Each cross (or dot) represents one electron.

You'll learn how to work out how many electron pairs there are around a central atom as part of your chemistry course.

3) Here's how to **draw** the **3D shapes** of different molecules using the rules you saw on the previous page:

Two Electron Pairs — Linear

1) If an atom has **two pairs of bonding electrons** around it and **no lone pairs**, the molecule will be **linear**.

2) The bonds in a linear molecule lie in a **straight line**. They're all in the **same plane**, so the molecule is **flat**.

$$180°$$
$$Cl—Be—Cl$$

$BeCl_2$ is a linear molecule.

$$180°$$
$$O=C=O$$

The double lines show a double bond. You can treat each double bond the same as one single bond, so CO_2 is linear too.

Three Electron Pairs — Trigonal Planar

1) If the central atom has **three pairs of bonding electrons** around it and **no lone pairs**, the molecule will be **trigonal planar**.

2) This means that it's in the shape of a **flat triangle**, with each of the bonds pointing towards one of the corners.

BF_3 is a trigonal planar molecule — the B is in the centre of the triangle, with one F at each corner.

Four Electron Pairs — Tetrahedral, Trigonal Pyramidal or Bent

1) If the central atom has **four pairs of bonding electrons** and **no lone pairs**, the molecule will be **tetrahedral**. A **tetrahedron** is a regular triangular-based pyramid.

2) The central atom sits in the **centre** of the pyramid, with a bond pointing out at each corner.

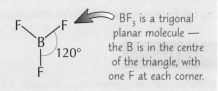

Methane (CH_4) is a tetrahedral molecule — the C is in the centre of the pyramid, with one H at each corner.

1) If the central atom has **three pairs of bonding electrons** and **one lone pair**, the molecule will be **trigonal pyramidal**.

2) Its shape is like a **triangular-based pyramid** with the lone pair of electrons sitting at the top.

Ammonia (NH_3) is a trigonal pyramidal molecule.

Trigonal pyramidal is also sometimes just called 'pyramidal'.

1) If the central atom has **two pairs of bonding electrons** and **two lone pairs**, the molecule is **bent** (or **non-linear**).

2) These molecules are **flat**, but their bonds **don't** lie in a straight line.

Water (H_2O) is a bent molecule.

Five Electron Pairs — Trigonal Bipyramidal

1) If the central atom has **five pairs of bonding electrons** around it and **no lone pairs**, the molecule will be **trigonal bipyramidal**.

2) This is a shape that's like two triangular-based pyramids whose bases have been stuck together.

3) The central atom sits in the **centre** of the shape, with each of the bonds pointing towards one of the corners.

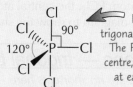

PCl_5 is trigonal bipyramidal. The P sits in the centre, with one Cl at each corner.

Drawing Molecules in 3D

Six Electron Pairs — Octahedral or Square Planar

1) If the central atom has **six pairs of bonding electrons**, the molecule will be **octahedral**.

2) An **octahedron** is a shape that's like two square-based pyramids whose bases have been stuck together.

3) The central atom sits in the **centre** of the octahedron, with each of the bonds pointing towards one of the corners.

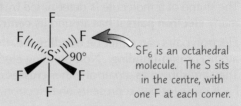

SF_6 is an octahedral molecule. The S sits in the centre, with one F at each corner.

1) If the central atom has **four pairs of bonding electrons** and **two lone pairs**, the molecule will be **square planar**.

2) This means that it's in the shape of a **flat square**, with each of the bonds pointing towards one of the corners.

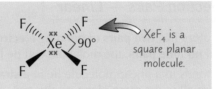

XeF_4 is a square planar molecule.

There are a few other less common shapes that are possible with different combinations of bonding and non-bonding pairs of electrons. It's best to check which shapes you'll need to know for the exam board you're studying.

If you're studying the full A-level course, you'll come across some of these shapes when you're learning about transition metal complexes too.

Worked Example

In the molecule carbon tetrachloride, CCl_4, carbon is the central atom.
It has four bonding pairs of electrons around it and no lone pairs of electrons.
Draw a diagram to show the shape of carbon tetrachloride. Name the shape that you have drawn.

1 *Work out what shape the molecule will be.*
Use the number of bonding pairs and lone pairs of electrons around the central atom to identify the shape of the molecule.

Four bonding pairs and no lone pairs = **tetrahedral**

2 *Sketch out the shape with the atoms in the right places.*
Make sure that you get the wedge bond and the dotted line bond in the right places.

3 *Label the bond angles in your diagram.*
The bond angles are an important part of the shape too.

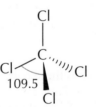

Practice Questions

Q1 State the name of the molecular shape shown in the diagram on the right.

Q2 The molecule sulfur dichloride, SCl_2, has two bonding pairs of electrons and two lone pairs around its central S atom. State what shape an SCl_2 molecule will be.

Q3 In the molecule BH_3, the central atom (B) has three bonding pairs of electrons and no lone pairs around it. Draw a diagram to show the shape of a molecule of BH_3. Name the shape that you have drawn.

Q4 In the atom PCl_3, the central atom (P) has three pairs of bonding electrons and one lone pair around it. Draw a diagram to show the shape of a PCl_3 atom. Name the shape that you have drawn.

Get in shape — trigonal bipyramidal looks like a fun one to me...

I'm afraid there are no shortcuts here — you've just got to know the diagrams of all the possible molecule shapes well enough to sketch them out. The good news is that once you know them, it all gets much easier. Then if you're asked to draw a molecule, all you have to do is work out what shape it will be and draw it out with the atoms in the right places.

Symmetry

Take a deep breath and prepare yourself for three pages on symmetry. The downside is that it's full of mirror lines and reflecting things. The upside is it's the last topic in the geometry section and only contains one dodgy reflection pun.

Objects that are **Symmetrical** Have **Mirror Lines**

(Some shapes have rotational symmetry too, but you don't need to worry about that here.)

If you can draw a **mirror line** through a shape, then it is described as **symmetrical**. If you fold the shape along the mirror line, the two sides will fit together exactly. For example, these shapes are symmetrical:

Shapes that do not have a line of symmetry are called 'unsymmetrical' or 'asymmetric'.

Molecules can be symmetrical too, for example:

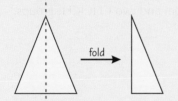
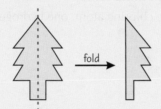
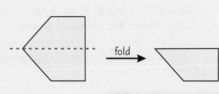
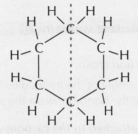

In all of these molecules, the arrangement of atoms on one side of the line of symmetry is the exact mirror images of the arrangement of atoms on the other side.

(These three molecules all have at least one other line of symmetry, besides the one shown.)

Symmetry is important in chemistry because whether or not an organic molecule is symmetrical will affect:

- how the molecule behaves in certain reactions,
- whether the molecule has **optical isomers** or not (see page 61).

Spotting **Symmetry** from a **Displayed Formula** can be **Tricky**

1) Often in chemistry, you won't be able to tell whether a molecule's symmetrical or not using mirror lines and its **displayed formula**.

2) A molecule that might look unsymmetrical at first glance might not actually be.

For example, if you were asked to draw the displayed formula of **1,2-dichloroethane**, you might draw it like this:

This **doesn't** look symmetrical.

$$Cl-\overset{\overset{\displaystyle H}{|}}{C}-\overset{\overset{\displaystyle Cl}{|}}{C}-H$$

But you can also draw the displayed formula like this:

You can see from this that it **is symmetrical**.

$$Cl-\overset{\overset{\displaystyle H}{|}}{\underset{\underset{\displaystyle H}{|}}{C}}-\overset{\overset{\displaystyle H}{|}}{\underset{\underset{\displaystyle H}{|}}{C}}-Cl$$

3) To work out if an organic molecule is symmetrical, you need to look at what **atoms** or **groups of atoms** are attached to the central atom or bond in the carbon chain:

1) Draw out the **displayed formula** of the molecule and find the bond or atom that sits in the middle of the carbon chain. ◄

2) If the middle of the chain is a **carbon atom**, look at what groups are attached to it. If at least two of the groups are the same, then the molecule is symmetrical.

If the middle of the chain is a **bond**, look at what groups are attached to the carbons at either end. If both carbons have exactly the same groups attached then the molecule is symmetrical.

If the molecule has an odd number of carbons in its chain, then the centre will be a carbon atom. If it has an even number of carbons in its chain, then the centre will be a bond.

Symmetry

Worked Example 1

Is the molecule 2,3,4-trichloropentane symmetrical?

1 *Find the centre of the carbon chain.*

Draw out the displayed formula of the molecule. The carbon chain is five carbons long, so the centre will be the third carbon atom.

$$
\begin{array}{ccccc}
H & Cl & Cl & Cl & H \\
| & | & | & | & | \\
H-C-&C-&C-&C-&C-H \\
| & | & | & | & | \\
H & H & H & H & H
\end{array}
$$

2 *Look at what groups are attached to the central carbon*

The central carbon atom is joined to one chlorine atom, one hydrogen atom and two $CHClCH_3$ groups. Two of these are identical groups, so:

> 2,3,4-trichloropentane is **symmetrical**.

Worked Example 2

Is the molecule 1,3-dichlorobutane symmetrical?

1 *Find the centre of the carbon chain.*

Draw out the displayed formula of the molecule. The carbon chain is four carbons long, so the centre will be the bond between the second and third carbon atoms.

$$
\begin{array}{cccc}
Cl & H & Cl & H \\
| & | & | & | \\
H-C-&C-&C-&C-H \\
| & | & | & | \\
H & H & H & H
\end{array}
$$

2 *Look at what groups are attached to the carbons at each end of the central bond.*

The second carbon atom is joined to two hydrogen atoms, one CH_2Cl group and one $CHClCH_3$ group. The third carbon atom is joined to one hydrogen atom, one chlorine atom, one CH_3 group and one CH_2CH_2Cl group. The two carbon atoms on either side of the central bond are attached to different groups, so:

> 1,3-dichlorobutane is **unsymmetrical**.

A *Chiral Carbon* has *Four Different Groups* Attached to it

A carbon atom in an organic molecule that has four different groups attached to it is called a **chiral carbon**.

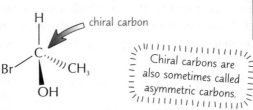

Chiral carbons are also sometimes called asymmetric carbons.

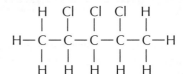

Choral carbon.

Worked Example 3

The molecule 1,1-dichloropropan-2-ol ($CHCl_2CHOHCH_3$) contains a chiral carbon atom. The displayed formula of 1,1-dichloropropan-2-ol is shown below on the right.

Mark the chiral carbon with an asterisk.

1 *Find the carbon atom with four different groups attached.*

- Carbon 1 has two Cl atoms, one H atom and one $CHOHCH_3$ group attached to it.
- Carbon 2 has one $CHCl_2$ group, one H atom, one OH group and one CH_3 group attached to it.
- Carbon 3 has three H atoms and one $CHCl_2CHOH$ group attached to it.

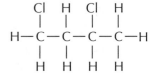

Carbon 2 is the only one to have four different groups attached to it — so carbon 2 is the chiral carbon.

2 *Mark the chiral carbon with an asterisk.*

Put an asterisk (a little star) next to the carbon atom that you identified in step 2.

$$
\begin{array}{ccc}
Cl & OH & H \\
| & | & | \\
H-C-&\overset{*}{C}-&C-H \\
| & | & | \\
Cl & H & H
\end{array}
$$

Symmetry

You Can Draw **3D Diagrams** to Show Pairs of **Optical Isomers**

1) Whenever you have a molecule with a chiral carbon, you can arrange the four groups around the carbon in two different ways — in other words a molecule with a chiral carbon has two different **isomers**.

2) The two possible isomers will be **mirror images** of each other.
   For example, this diagram shows the two possible isomers of bromochloroiodomethane:

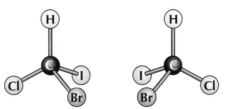

> The right-hand image is a reflection of the left-hand one.

3) These isomers are called **optical isomers**, or **enantiomers**.

4) Here's how to draw a 3D diagram showing a pair of enantiomers:

Worked Example 4

The molecule 1-bromo-1-chloropropane has two enantiomers.
The displayed formula of 1-bromo-1-chloropropane is shown on the right.
The chiral carbon is marked with an asterisk.
Draw the two enantiomers of 1-bromo-1-chloropropane.

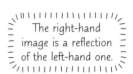

1-bromo-1-chloropropane

1 *Draw out the molecule in a tetrahedral shape.*

Draw out the basic shape of a **tetrahedral** molecule (see page 57) with the **chiral carbon** in the middle.
Then add the other three groups to the ends of the bonds (it doesn't matter where each of the other groups go).

2 *Draw a mirror line next to the first molecule.*

3 *Use the mirror line to draw the mirror image of the first molecule beside it.*

Use the mirror line to draw out the reflection of the first molecule in the mirror line.

The two molecules you have drawn are the two enantiomers of 1-bromo-1-chloropropane.

The 'wedge', 'dotted' and 'line' bonds are on the opposite sides.

The left and right-hand groups have swapped sides.

Practice Questions

Q1 Work out whether each of the following molecules is symmetrical or unsymmetrical.
   a) 2,3-dichloropentane, $CH_3CHClCHClCH_2CH_3$.
   b) 2,5-dimethylhexane, $CH_3CHCH_3CH_2CH_2CHCH_3CH_3$.

Q2 The molecule 2-chlorobutane contains a chiral carbon.
   a) The displayed formula of 2-chlorobutane is shown on the right. Mark the chiral carbon with an asterisk (*).
   b) Draw the two possible enantiomers of 2-chlorobutane.

All this symmetry is melting my mind... ...bnim ym gnitlem si yrtemmys siht llA

On reflection (ho, ho, ho...) symmetry's not such a bad topic. The main thing that's going to help here is practising the methods. So get plenty of practice at spotting symmetrical molecules, finding chiral carbons and drawing out pairs of enantiomers. Then when you've got it nailed, give yourself a mirror high-five. Carefully though, seven years bad luck and all...

Answers

Section 1 — Calculations

Page 5 — Rounding and Decimal Places

1 a) 0.027 g s^{-1}
  b) 11.33 dm^3
  c) 24.0 kJ
  d) 0.92 V
2   325 g $= (325 \div 1000)$ kg $= 0.325$ kg
    80 minutes $= (80 \div 60)$ hours $= 1.333...$ hours
    So the rate $= 0.325 \div 1.333...$
        $= 0.24375$ kg hour^{-1}
        $= \mathbf{0.24}$ **kg hour^{-1} (2 d.p.)**

Page 7 — Significant Figures

1 a) 6
  b) 3
    This could have 4 or 5 significant figures — but you can only say
    for sure that it has 3.
  c) 4
    Remember, zeros after the decimal point *do* count as significant figures
    (as long as they come after non-zero digits).
  d) 3
2 a) 650 kJ
  b) 649 kJ
  c) 649.4 kJ
3    $0.175 \div 1.2 = 0.145833...$ mol dm^{-3}
        $= \mathbf{0.15}$ **mol dm^{-3} (to 2 s.f.)**
    The volume of water (1.2 dm^3) is the data value with the fewest number
    of significant figures in this calculation — it's given to two significant
    figures, so you should round the final answer to two significant figures too.

Page 9 — Standard Form

1   3.5×10^{-5} mol dm^{-3}
2    $215\,000$ Pa
3   number of moles $=$ (concentration $\times$ volume in cm^3) $\div 1000$
        $= (6.3 \times 10^{-5} \times 75) \div 1000$
        $= 4.725 \times 10^{-6}$
        $= \mathbf{4.7 \times 10^{-6}}$ **mol dm^{-3} (to 2 s.f.)**
4 a) Divide the volume in dm^3 by 1000 to convert to m^3:
    $(6.85 \times 10^{12}) \div 1000 = \mathbf{6.85 \times 10^{9}}$ **m^3**
  b) Multiply the volume in dm^3 by 1000 to convert to cm^3:
    $(6.85 \times 10^{12}) \times 1000 = \mathbf{6.85 \times 10^{15}}$ **cm^3**
5   number of atoms $=$ total mass $\div$ mass of one atom
        $= 25 \div (3.82 \times 10^{-23})$
        $= 6.5445... \times 10^{23} = \mathbf{6.5 \times 10^{23}}$ **atoms (to 2 s.f.)**

Page 11 — Fractions

1    $\frac{187.5}{256.0} \times 100\% = (187.5 \div 256.0) \times 100\%$
        $= 0.73242... \times 100\%$
        $= \mathbf{73.24\%}$ **(to 4 s.f.)**
2    $\frac{0.020 \times 50}{1000} = (0.020 \times 50) \div 1000$
        $= 1.0 \div 1000$
        $= \mathbf{0.0010}$ **mol dm^{-3} (to 2 s.f.)**
    Remember, you should give your answer to the same number of
    significant figures as the data value that has the fewest significant figures
    in the calculation. Zeros that come after a decimal point are significant,
    so 0.20 mol dm^{-3} and 50 cm^3 are both given to 2 s.f. — this means
    you should give your answer to 2 s.f.
3 a) $n = \frac{pV}{RT}$

    $= \frac{160\,000 \times 0.50}{8.31 \times 450}$

    $= (160\,000 \times 0.50) \div (8.31 \times 450)$
    $= 80\,000 \div 3739.5$
    $= 21.39... = \mathbf{21}$ **moles (to 2. s.f.)**

  b) $n = \frac{pV}{RT}$

    $= \frac{225\,000 \times 0.35}{8.31 \times (80 + 273)}$
    $= (225\,000 \times 0.35) \div (8.31 \times (80 + 273))$
    $= (225\,000 \times 0.35) \div (8.31 \times 353)$
    $= 78\,750 \div 2933.43$
    $= 26.84... = \mathbf{27}$ **moles (to 2. s.f.)**

Page 13 — Percentages

1 a) Find 8.80 g out of 10.0 g as a percentage:
    $8.80 \div 10.0 = 0.880$
    $0.880 \times 100 = \mathbf{88.0\%}$
  b) Find 88.0% of 16.0 g:
    $88.0 \div 100 = 0.880$
    $0.880 \times 16.0 = 14.08 = \mathbf{14.1}$ **g (to 3 s.f.)**
2 a) $100\% - 85.7\% = \mathbf{14.3\%}$
  b) 24.6 g $= 85.7\%$
    So 100% is $(24.6 \div 85.7) \times 100 = 0.2870... \times 100$
        $= \mathbf{28.7}$ **g (to 3 s.f.)**
  c) Find 14.3% of 35.0 g:
    $14.3 \div 100 = 0.143$
    $0.143 \times 35.0 = 5.005 = \mathbf{5.01}$ **g (to 3 s.f.)**

Page 15 — Ratios

1 a) E.g. $6 : 12 : 6$ (or any equivalent ratio)
  b) All the numbers in the molecular formula divide by 6:
    $6 : 12 : 6 = 1 : 2 : 1$.
    This is the ratio in its simplest form,
    so the empirical formula of glucose is $\mathbf{CH_2O}$.
2   The ratio of C : H : O is $2 : 4 : 1$.
    To get an equivalent ratio with 3 oxygens,
    multiply everything in the ratio by 3:
    $2 : 4 : 1 = (2 \times 3) : (4 \times 3) : (1 \times 3) = 6 : 12 : 3$
    So the molecular formula is $\mathbf{C_6H_{12}O_3}$.
3   The ratio of carbon dioxide : water is $3 : 4$.
    You could write this the other way round, i.e. say the ratio of water to
    carbon dioxide is 4 : 3. If you did this, you'd need to flip all the other
    ratios in the question round too.
    Divide both sides by 4 to find how many moles of carbon
    dioxide would be made from 1 mole of water:
    $(3 \div 4) : (4 \div 4) = 0.75 : 1$
    Multiply both sides by 22 to find how many moles of
    carbon dioxide would be made from 22 moles of water:
    $(0.75 \times 22) : (1 \times 22) = 16.5 : 22$
    So the reaction made **16.5 moles** of carbon dioxide.
4   The ratio of sulfur : fluorine : chlorine
    is $0.0308 : 0.154 : 0.0308$.
    Divide by the smallest number in the ratio (0.0308)
    to get the ratio into its simplest form:
    S: $\frac{0.0308}{0.0308} = 1.00$, F: $\frac{0.154}{0.0308} = 5.00$, Cl: $\frac{0.0308}{0.0308} = 1.00$
    The ratio of S : F : Cl in the compound is $1 : 5 : 1$.
    So the empirical formula is $\mathbf{SF_5Cl}$.

Page 17 — Estimating and Predicting

1 a) E.g. 20 seconds
    You don't want to end up with too many data points, or too few.
    15, 20 or 30 seconds are all sensible suggestions here.
  b) E.g. 0.01 g
    The overall change in mass is very small here so measurements to the
    nearest 1 g definitely won't be any good. If the rate of the reaction is
    slow at the start or end of the experiment, even the nearest 0.1 g might
    not be accurate enough, so the nearest 0.01 g is a safer bet.
2   If a smaller proportion of PCl_5 dissociates, there will be more
    PCl_5 and less PCl_3 and Cl_2. If $[PCl_5]$ increases and $[PCl_3]$ and
    $[Cl_2]$ decrease, then the value of K_c will decrease.

Answers

Page 19 — Powers

1   $6.02 \times 10^{23} \times 10^5 = 6.02 \times 10^{23 + 5}$
$$= \mathbf{6.02 \times 10^{28}}$$

2   $K_c = (0.60^3 \times 0.20) \div 0.40^2 = (0.216 \times 0.20) \div 0.16$
$$= \mathbf{0.27 \ mol^2 \ dm^{-6}}$$

3   Rate $= k[A][B] = (1.12 \times 10^4) \times (1.96 \times 10^{-4}) \times (1.84 \times 10^{-2})$
$$= 1.12 \times 1.96 \times 1.84 \times 10^4 \times 10^{-4} \times 10^{-2}$$
$$= 4.039168 \times 10^{(4 + -4 + -2)}$$
$$= 4.039168 \times 10^{-2}$$
$$= \mathbf{4.04 \times 10^{-2} \ mol \ dm^{-3} \ s^{-1} \ (to \ 3 \ s.f.)}$$
If you need a reminder about standard form, have a look at pages 8-9.
If you need a reminder about significant figures, have a look at pages 6-7.

Page 21 — Logarithms

1   $pK_a = -\log_{10}(K_a)$
$$= -\log_{10}(3.5 \times 10^{-8})$$
$$= 7.45593... = \mathbf{7.46 \ (to \ 2 \ d.p)}$$

2 a) $pH = -\log_{10} 0.025$
$$= 1.602... = \mathbf{1.60 \ (to \ 2 \ d.p.)}$$

   b) $pH = -\log_{10} (7.9 \times 10^{-14})$
$$= 13.102... = \mathbf{13.10 \ (to \ 2 \ d.p.)}$$

   c) $[H^+] = 10^{-pH}$
$$= 10^{-4.80}$$
$$= 1.58489... \times 10^{-5} = \mathbf{1.6 \times 10^{-5} \ (to \ 2 \ s.f.)}$$

   d) $[H^+] = 10^{-pH}$
$$= 10^{-5.23}$$
$$= 5.8884... \times 10^{-6} = \mathbf{5.8 \times 10^{-6} \ (to \ 2 \ s.f.)}$$

Don't forget about the special significant figure rules for logs for these questions. Round log x to the same number of decimal places as there are significant figures in x. Round 10^y to the same number of significant figures as y has decimal places.

3   In order to find the pH of the solution, you need to know its hydrogen ion concentration. So first rearrange the K_w expression to find $[H^+]$:
$K_w = [H^+][OH^-]$
$[H^+] = K_w \div [OH^-]$
Now substitute in the numbers from the question:
$[H^+] = (1.00 \times 10^{-14}) \div 0.631 = 1.5847... \times 10^{-14} \ mol \ dm^{-3}$
Finally, put the $[H^+]$ value into the pH formula:
$pH = -\log_{10}[H^+]$
$= -\log_{10}(1.5847... \times 10^{-14})$
$= 13.8000.... = \mathbf{13.800 \ (to \ 3 \ d.p.)}$
This question looks tricky, but if you take it step by step it's not too bad — it's just a question of working out that you need $[H^+]$ to calculate pH, and then working out how you can find $[H^+]$ from the data you've got.

Page 23 — Natural Logs

1   $k = Ae^{\frac{-E_a}{RT}}$
$$= (5.02 \times 10^9) \times e^{\frac{-122\,000}{8.31 \times 345}}$$
$$= (5.02 \times 10^9) \times e^{\frac{-122\,000}{2866.95}}$$
$$= (5.02 \times 10^9) \times e^{-42.5539...}$$
$$= (5.02 \times 10^9) \times (3.30416... \times 10^{-19})$$
$$= 1.6586... \times 10^{-9} = \mathbf{1.66 \times 10^{-9} \ s^{-1} \ (to \ 3 \ s.f.)}$$

2 a) $\ln k = \ln A - \dfrac{E_a}{RT}$

    $\dfrac{E_a}{RT} = \ln A - \ln k$ (First add $\frac{E_a}{RT}$ to both sides, and subtract ln k.)

    $\dfrac{E_a}{RT} = \ln\left(\dfrac{A}{k}\right)$ (Now use the rule $\ln\left(\frac{x}{y}\right) = \ln(x) - \ln(y)$ to simplify the right hand side.)

    $E_a = RT \times \ln\left(\dfrac{A}{k}\right)$ (Finally, multiply both sides by RT.)

   b) $E_a = 8.31 \times 375 \times \ln\left(\dfrac{8.41 \times 10^{11}}{1.83 \times 10^{-5}}\right)$
$$= 8.31 \times 375 \times \ln (4.5956... \times 10^{16})$$
$$= 8.31 \times 375 \times 38.366...$$
$$= 119\,559.50... = \mathbf{120\,000 \ J \ mol^{-1} \ (to \ 3 \ s.f.)}$$

3   Rearrange $\ln k = \ln A - \dfrac{E_a}{RT}$ to make T the subject.

   $\dfrac{E_a}{RT} + \ln k = \ln A$

   $\dfrac{E_a}{RT} = \ln A - \ln k$

   $\dfrac{E_a}{R} = T(\ln A - \ln k)$

   $T = \dfrac{E_a}{R} \div (\ln A - \ln k) = \dfrac{E_a}{R(\ln A - \ln k)}$

Now substitute in the numbers from the question:

   $T = \dfrac{367\,000}{8.31 \times (\ln(1.21 \times 10^{10}) - \ln(0.00710))}$

   $T = \dfrac{367\,000}{8.31 \times (23.21647... - (-4.94766...))}$

   $T = \dfrac{367\,000}{8.31 \times 28.1641...} = \dfrac{367\,000}{234.0439...}$

   $T = 1568.08... = \mathbf{1570 \ K \ (to \ 3 \ s.f.)}$

You might well have used a slightly different method to answer this question from the one that's shown here — for example you might have rearranged the equation in a different way, or you could even have substituted the numbers into the formula first and then rearranged it. As long as you ended up with the right value of T, you're fine.

Section 2 — Units
Page 26 — Using Units

1   concentration $= 0.35 \div 0.07 = 5$
units of concentration $= g \div dm^3 = g \ dm^{-3}$
rate $= \mathbf{5 \ g \ dm^{-3}}$

2   rate $= 15 \div 6.0 = 2.5$
units of rate $= g \div min = g \ min^{-1}$
rate $= \mathbf{2.5 \ g \ min^{-1}}$

3   $K_p = \dfrac{p_{N_2O_4}}{(p_{NO_2})^2}$

Units of $K_p = \dfrac{kPa}{(kPa)^2}$

$$= \dfrac{kPa}{kPa \times kPa}$$

Cancelling units gives $K_p = \dfrac{\cancel{kPa}}{kPa \times \cancel{kPa}} = \dfrac{1}{kPa}$

To remove the fraction, make all positive powers on the bottom of the fraction negative, and all negative powers positive.
So units of $K_p = \mathbf{kPa^{-1}}$

4 a)   rate $= k[NO]^2$

    $k = \dfrac{rate}{[NO]^2}$

    units of $k = \dfrac{mol \ dm^{-3} \ s^{-1}}{(mol \ dm^{-3})^2}$

    units of $k = \dfrac{\cancel{mol \ dm^{-3}} \ s^{-1}}{(mol \ dm^{-3})(\cancel{mol \ dm^{-3}})} = \dfrac{s^{-1}}{mol \ dm^{-3}}$

    units of $k = \mathbf{mol^{-1} \ dm^3 \ s^{-1}}$

   b)   rate $= k[C(CH_3)_3I]$

    $k = \dfrac{rate}{[C(CH_3)_3I]}$

    units of $k = \dfrac{mol \ dm^{-3} \ s^{-1}}{mol \ dm^{-3}}$

    units of $k = \dfrac{\cancel{mol \ dm^{-3}} \ s^{-1}}{\cancel{mol \ dm^{-3}}} = \dfrac{s^{-1}}{1}$

    units of $k = \mathbf{s^{-1}}$

Answers

c) rate = k[NO]^2[H$_2$]

$$k = \frac{rate}{[NO]^2[H_2]}$$

units of $k = \dfrac{mol\,dm^{-3}\,s^{-1}}{(mol\,dm^{-3})^2(mol\,dm^{-3})}$

units of $k = \dfrac{\cancel{mol}\,dm^{-3}\,s^{-1}}{(mol\,dm^{-3})^2\cancel{(mol\,dm^{-3})}} = \dfrac{s^{-1}}{(mol\,dm^{-3})^2}$

units of $k = \dfrac{s^{-1}}{(mol\,dm^{-3})(mol\,dm^{-3})} = \dfrac{s^{-1}}{mol^2\,dm^{-6}}$

units of $k =$ **mol^{-2} dm^6 s^{-1}**

Page 29 — Converting Units

1 a) 240 g = (240 ÷ 1000) kg
      = **0.240 kg**
   b) 4.1 kJ mol^{-1} = (4.1 × 1000) J mol^{-1}
        = **4100 J mol^{-1}**
   c) 0.5 dm^3 = (0.5 × 1000) cm^3
      = **500 cm^3**

2 4.6 min = (4.6 × 60) s
      = **276 s**

3 0.025 dm^3 = (0.025 × 1000) cm^3
       = 25 cm^3
   Total volume = 31 cm^3 + 25 cm^3
       = **56 cm^3**

Section 3 — Handling Data

Page 31 — Tables of Data

1 a) 12.50 cm^3
   b) Run 2
   c) 12.25 cm^3
    This question is just asking you to find the smallest value in the table.
   d) 36.75 + 38.00 + 37.75 = **112.5 cm^3**
    For this question, you just need to add up the volumes
    for each of the three runs in the 0.3 mol dm^{-3} row.

Page 33 — Finding the Mean

1 a) $\dfrac{15.7 + 16.5 + 16.0}{3} = 48.2 \div 3$
          = 16.066... = **16.1 g (to 3 s.f.)**
    Remember, all of the data in the question is given to
    3 significant figures, so the answer should be too.

2 a) Repeat 4 (−1869 kJ mol^{-1})
    This value is quite a lot lower than the others,
    so it looks like this is where the mistake happened.
   b) $\dfrac{(-2866) + ((-2879) + (-2876) + (-2888))}{4}$
    =11509 ÷ 4
    = 2877.25 = **2877 kJ mol^{-1} (to 4 s.f.)**

3 a) $\dfrac{55.40 + 55.40 + 55.50 + 55.50}{4}$
    = 221.80 ÷ 4
    = **55.45 cm^3**
   b) $\dfrac{27.20 + 27.25 + 27.15}{3}$
    = 81.60 ÷ 3
    = **27.20 cm^3**
   c) Including the anomalous result (run 3) would make the value
   of the mean lower than it should be.
    Run three is a lot smaller than all of the other runs,
    so including it would decrease the value of the mean.

Page 35 — The Mean and Relative Atomic Mass

1 (20.0 × 10.0) = 200   (80.0 × 11.0) = 880
   200 + 880 =1080
   1080 ÷ 100 = **10.8**

2 No, the student is not correct. As the relative atomic mass of
   carbon isn't a whole number, carbon must have at least two
   isotopes with different abundances.

3 (180.5 × 85) = 15 342.5   (67.5 × 87) = 5872.5
   15 342.5 + 5872.5 = 21215
   21 215 ÷ (180.5 + 67.5) = 21 389 ÷ 248
          = 85.544... = **85.5 (to 3 s.f.)**

Page 37 — Uncertainty and Error

1 Uncertainty = 1 cm^3 ÷ 2 = **±0.5 cm^3**

2 a) Percentage uncertainty = $\dfrac{uncertainty}{reading} \times 100$
          = $\dfrac{0.01}{0.25} \times 100$
          = **4%**
   b) E.g. the student could weigh out a larger amount
   of the compound.

3 uncertainty = (percentage uncertainty ÷ 100) × reading
       = (5% ÷ 100) × 0.41
       = 0.05 × 0.41
       = ±0.0205 = **±0.021 V (to 2 s.f.)**
   If you can't remember how to get from 'percentage uncertainty' back
   to 'uncertainty' off the top of your head, you could always write down
   the percentage uncertainty formula and then rearrange it.

4 E.g. the percentage uncertainty using flask A is ±1%.
   The percentage uncertainty using of flask B is
   $\dfrac{0.1}{150} \times 100 = 0.0666... = 0.07\%$ (to 1 s.f.)

   0.07% is less than 1%, so the student should use **flask B**.
   Since the student would be measuring out the same volume of liquid
   in either flask here, you could have found the uncertainty on a
   measurement in flask A (±1.5 cm^3) instead.

Page 39 — Combining Uncertainties

1 Temperature change = 45.6 − 20.4 = 25.2 °C
   Total uncertainty = 0.2 + 0.2 = 0.4 °C
   Temperature change = **25.2 ±0.4 °C**

2 Change in pH = 7.5 − 5.9 = 1.6
   Total uncertainty = 0.1+ 0.1 = 0.2
   Change in pH = **1.6 ±0.2**

3 Mass of CaCl$_2$ added to flask = 55.0 − 30.0
           = 25.0 g
   Uncertainty of bottle + CaCl$_2$ = (0.91 × 55.0) ÷ 100
           = ±0.5005 g
   Uncertainty of empty bottle = (1.67 × 30.0) ÷ 100
          = ±0.501 g
   Total uncertainty for mass of CaCl$_2$ = 0.5005 + 0.501
           = ±1.0015 g
   Mass of CaCl$_2$ added to flask = **25.0 g ±1.0 g**
   Remember, you should only give the uncertainty to the same accuracy
   as the calculated measurement.

4 Total uncertainty = 0.1 + 0.1 + 0.2 + 0.2
        = 0.6 cm^3
   Volume added from burette A = 25.2 − 1.2
         = 24 cm^3
   Volume added from burette B = 5.6 − 2.6
         = 3 cm^3
   Total volume added = 24 + 3
        = 27 cm^3
   Percentage uncertainty = (0.6 ÷ 27) × 100
         = 2.222... = **2.2% (to 2 s.f)**

Answers

Section 4 — Equations and Formulae

Page 41 — Using Equations and Formulae

1 $n = m \div M_r$
   $m = 125$ g and $M_r = 44.0$.
   number of moles of $CO_2 = 125 \div 44.0$
   $\qquad\qquad = 2.8409... = \textbf{2.84 (3 s.f.)}$

2 Concentration = number of moles ÷ volume,
   number of moles of $CaCl_2 = 5.0$,
   volume of water = 750 cm^3
   $\qquad\qquad = (750 \div 1000)$ dm^3
   $\qquad\qquad = 0.75$ dm^3,
   So concentration $= 5.0 \div 0.75$
   $\qquad\qquad = 6.666... = \textbf{6.7 mol dm}^3 \textbf{ (2 s.f.)}$

3 a) $q = mc\Delta T$
   $m = 104$ g, $c = 4.18$ $J\,g^{-1}\,K^{-1}$ and $\Delta T = 361 - 298 = 63$ K
   So $q = 104 \times 4.18 \times 63$
   $\qquad = 27387.36$ J
   $\qquad = (27387.36 \div 1000)$ kJ
   $\qquad = 27.387...$ kJ $= \textbf{27.4 kJ (3 s.f.)}$

  b) $n = m \div M_r$
   $m = 16.0$ g and $M_r = 64.0$.
   number of moles of X $= 16.0 \div 64.0$
   $\qquad\qquad = \textbf{0.250 moles}$

  c) $\Delta H_c = 27.387... \div 0.25$
   $\qquad = 109.549... = \textbf{110 kJ mol}^{-1} \textbf{ (3 s.f.)}$

Page 45 — Rearranging Equations

1 concentration $= \dfrac{\text{number of moles}}{\text{volume}}$
   Multiply both sides by volume:
   concentration × volume = number of moles
   Divide by concentration:
   volume $= \dfrac{\text{number of moles}}{\text{concentration}}$
   number of moles $= 2.5 \times 10^{-3}$
   concentration $= 7.5 \times 10^{-3}$ $mol\,dm^{-3}$
   volume $= (2.5 \times 10^{-3}) \div (7.5 \times 10^{-3})$
   $\qquad = 0.33... = \textbf{0.33 dm}^3 \textbf{ (2 s.f.)}$

2 $pV = nRT$
   Divide both sides by p:
   $V = \dfrac{nRT}{p}$
   $n = 5.6$ moles, $R = 8.31$ $J\,K^{-1}\,mol^{-1}$
   $T = 350$ K and $p = 12\,000$ Pa.
   $V = \dfrac{5.6 \times 8.31 \times 350}{12\,000} = \dfrac{16\,287.6}{12\,000}$
   $\qquad\qquad = 1.3573$ $m^3 = \textbf{1.4 m}^3 \textbf{ (2 s.f.)}$

3 $K_c = \dfrac{[HI]^2}{[H_2][I_2]}$
   Multiply both sides by $[H_2]$:
   $K_c[H_2] = \dfrac{[HI]^2}{[I_2]}$
   Multiply both sides by $[I_2]$:
   $K_c[H_2][I_2] = [HI]^2$
   Take the square root of both sides:
   $\sqrt{K_c[H_2][I_2]} = \sqrt{[HI]^2} = [HI]$
   $K_c = 45.9$, $[H_2] = 0.228$ $mol\,dm^{-3}$
   $[I_2] = 0.228$ $mol\,dm^{-3}$
   $[HI] = \sqrt{45.9 \times 0.228 \times 0.228}$
   $\qquad = 1.544689... = \textbf{1.54 (3 s.f.)}$

Section 5 — Graph Skills

Page 48 — Plotting Graphs

1 a) time
  b) pH

2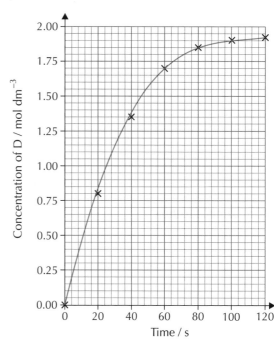

It's OK if you plotted your graph using a different scale to this, just as long as your scale is sensible.

Page 51 — Interpreting Graphs

1 a) The temperature stays constant until 20 seconds into the experiment and then increases to a maximum of 76 °C, before decreasing to around 67 °C after 75 seconds.
  b) Read up from 65 s on the x-axis to the line of best fit. Then read across to the y-axis:

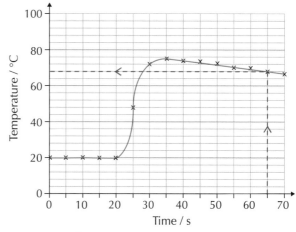

Temperature of reaction mixture at 65 s = **68 °C**

Answers

2 a) negative correlation

b) Extrapolate the line of best fit.
Read up from 276 s on the x-axis to the line of best fit.
Then read across to the y-axis:

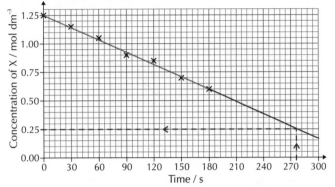

After 276 s, concentration of reactant X = **0.25 mol dm⁻³**

Page 53 — Linear Graphs

1 a) At the start of the reaction there is none of chemical Z present, but its concentration increases as the reaction continues.
So Z must be a product of the reaction.

b) To find the rate of the reaction, calculate the gradient of the graph, e.g.:

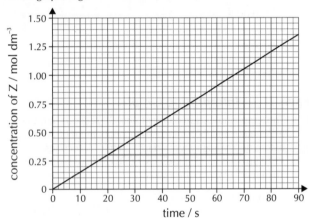

change in y = 1.05 − 0.30 = 0.75 mol dm⁻³
change in x = 70 − 20 = 50 s
gradient = $\dfrac{\text{change in } y}{\text{change in } x}$
= 0.75 ÷ 50
= **0.015 mol dm⁻³ s⁻¹**

You could have used a different bit of the graph to calculate the gradient, but you should still have got the same answer.

Page 55 — Curved Graphs and Tangents

1 The rate of reaction at time = 1 minute is the gradient of the tangent to the curve at time = 1 minute.
Draw tangents to both lines at time = 1 minute, e.g.:

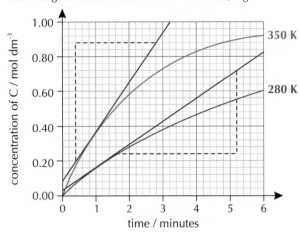

At 280 K (pink tangent):
change in y = 0.72 mol dm⁻³ − 0.24 mol dm⁻³
= 0.48 mol dm⁻³
change in x = 5.2 min − 1.6 min
= 3.6 min

gradient = $\dfrac{\text{change in } y}{\text{change in } x}$

= 0.48 ÷ 3.6
= 0.133... = **0.13 mol dm⁻³ min⁻¹ (to 2 s.f.)**

At 350 K (green tangent):
change in y = 0.88 mol dm⁻³ − 0.20 mol dm⁻³
= 0.68 mol dm⁻³
change in x = 2.8 min − 0.4 min
= 2.4 min

gradient = $\dfrac{\text{change in } y}{\text{change in } x}$

= 0.68 ÷ 2.4 = 0.283...
= **0.28 mol dm⁻³ min⁻¹ (to 2 s.f.)**

If you drew your tangents ever so slightly differently to the ones shown here, you might have got slightly different final answers too. As long as you calculated both answers correctly from sensibly drawn tangents, you're fine.

Section 6 — Geometry

Page 58 — Drawing Molecules in 3D

1 octahedral

2 bent / non-linear

3
$$H\diagdown \quad \diagup H$$
B
120°
H

trigonal planar

Don't forget to include the bond angle in your diagram — that counts as part of the shape too.

4
xx
P
Cl⁴⁴⁴⁴⁴ | ＼Cl
107°
Cl

trigonal pyramidal / pyramidal

Answers

Page 61 — Symmetry

1 a) Unsymmetrical

Here's how you'd work this one out:
Draw out the displayed formula of 2,3-dichloropentane.

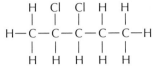

The carbon chain is five carbons long, so the centre is the third carbon atom. The central carbon atom is joined to one chlorine atom, one hydrogen atom, one CH_3CHCl group and one CH_2CH_3 group. None of these groups are the same, so the molecule is not symmetrical.

b) Symmetrical

And here's how you'd work this one out:
Draw out the displayed formula of 2,5-dimethylhexane.

The carbon chain is six carbons long, so the centre is the bond between the third and fourth carbon atoms.
The third carbon atom is joined to two hydrogen atoms, one $CHCH_3CH_3$ group and one $CH_2CHCH_3CH_3$ group.
The fourth carbon atom is joined to two hydrogen atoms, one $CHCH_3CH_3$ group and one $CH_2CHCH_3CH_3$ group.
The carbon atoms are attached to identical groups, so the molecule is symmetrical.

2 a)

And, finally, here's how you'd work this one out:
Look at what groups each of the carbon atoms is joined to.
Carbon 1 is joined to three Hs and a $CHClCH_2CH_3$ group.
Carbon 2 is joined to one H, one Cl, one CH_3 and a CH_2CH_3 group.
Carbon 3 is joined to two Hs, one CH_3 and a $CHClCH_3$ group.
Carbon 4 is joined to three Hs and a $CH_2CHClCH_3$ group.
So carbon 2 must be the chiral carbon (as it has four different groups).

b) E.g.

It doesn't matter if you put the different groups in different places around the chiral carbon in the 3D shape. As long as you've drawn a tetrahedral shape with the chiral carbon in the centre (with the correct four groups around it) and reflected it accurately in a mirror line, you'll have drawn the two enantiomers.

Glossary

A

Anomalous result
A result that doesn't fit in with the pattern of the other results in a set of data.

Asymmetric
A shape is asymmetric if it has no lines of symmetry (and no rotational symmetry). Asymmetric means the same as unsymmetrical.

B

Bond angle
The angle, in degrees, between two bonds in a molecule.

C

Causal relationship
A relationship between two variables where changing one variable causes the other to change.

Chiral carbon
Any carbon atom in an organic molecule that has four different groups attached to it.

Conversion factor
The number that you multiply or divide by in order to change from one unit to another.

Correlation
A description of how one variable changes as the other changes.

D

Dependent variable
The variable that you measure in an experiment.

Displayed formula
A displayed formula shows how the atoms in a molecule are arranged, with the covalent bonds between them shown as straight lines.

E

e
A mathematical constant. e is an irrational number, so it has an infinite number of decimal places. It has a value of 2.71828 when rounded to five decimal places.

Enantiomers
Two molecules, each containing a chiral carbon, that are exact mirror images of each other. Also called optical isomers.

Equation
A mathematical statement containing an equals sign which tells you that two mathematical expressions are equal.

Error
The amount by which a measurement that you have taken could be wrong — see also 'uncertainty'.

Exponential function
The mathematical constant 'e' raised to any power (often written as e^x).

Extrapolation
A technique where the trend in a set of data is used to estimate the value of a point that lies outside the range covered by the data set.

F

Formula
A mathematical statement that shows you the relationship between two or more variables.

G

Gradient
A measure of how steep a line on a graph is. Represented by m in the equation $y = mx + c$.

I

Independent variable
The variable that you change in an experiment.

Interpolation
A technique where the trend in a set of data is used to estimate the value of a point that lies within the range covered by the data set.

Inverse
The inverse of a function is its opposite. If you apply a function to a number and then apply the inverse to the answer, you get back to the original number.

Isomer
A molecule that has the same molecular formula as another molecule, but with the atoms connected in a different way.

L

Line of best fit
A line drawn on a scatter graph that fits the general pattern of the data and that passes as close to as many of the points as possible.

Linear graph
A graph which is a single straight line. The equation of a linear graph can always be written in the form $y = mx + c$.

Logarithm
The logarithm of a number tells you the power that the base must be raised to in order to give that number. So $\log_a y = x$ means $a^x = y$.

M

Mean
The average value of a data set, calculated by adding together all of the values in the set and then dividing the total by the number of values in the data set.

N

Natural logarithm
A logarithm with a base of e, where e is a constant with a value of 2.71828 to five decimal places.

Glossary

Optical isomer
Two molecules, each containing a chiral carbon, that are exact mirror images of each other. Also called enantiomers.

Percentage
A number written as an amount out of 100.

Percentage Uncertainty (or Percentage Error)
The uncertainty in a measurement given as a percentage of the measurement.

Power
A way of showing repeated multiplication. A power shows how many times its base should be multiplied by itself.

Precision
The smaller the spread of your data around the mean value, the more precise it is.

Prefix
A word that you can add in front of the name of a unit to make a larger or smaller unit. For example, adding kilo- to grams gives kilograms.

Ratio
A way of comparing two or more quantities. If you have 1 unit of A for every 2 units of B, then the ratio of A to B can be written as 1 : 2.

Relative atomic mass (A_r)
The mean mass of one atom of an element, on a scale where the mass of one atom of carbon-12 is exactly 12.

Scatter graph
A graph where data points are plotted with a dependent variable on one axis and an independent variable on the other axis.

Significant figure
A digit within a value that you are confident is correct (as opposed to a digit that you can't be sure about).

Standard form
A shorter way of writing very large or very small numbers that contain lots of zeros, by showing them as a number between 1 and 10, multiplied by a power of 10.

Symmetrical
A shape is symmetrical if it has a line of symmetry, i.e. a mirror line (or if it has rotational symmetry).

Tangent (to a curve)
A straight line that touches a curve at a single point but does not pass through it, and which has the same gradient as the curve at that point.

Uncertainty
An interval in which the true value of a measurement is likely to lie.

Unit
A set value of a measurement to which other quantities of the same type of measurement can be directly compared.

Unsymmetrical
A shape is unsymmetrical if it has no lines of symmetry (and no rotational symmetry). Unsymmetrical means the same as asymmetric

Variable
A quantity in an experiment, investigation or formula that can change or be changed.

Weighted mean
A special type of mean that takes into account the "importance" of each value in a data set when finding the average.

X

x-axis
The horizontal axis of a graph.

Y

y-axis
The vertical axis of a graph.

y-intercept
The point on a linear graph where the line crosses the y-axis ($x = 0$ at this point). Represented by c in the equation $y = mx + c$.

Index